Farmall Cub
& Cub Cadet

Kenneth Updike

MOTORBOOKS
INTERNATIONAL

This edition first published in 2002 by Motorbooks International, an imprint of MBI Publishing Company, Galtier Plaza, Suite 200, 380 Jackson Street, St. Paul, MN 55101-3885 USA

Motorbooks International titles are also available at discounts in bulk quantity for industrial or sales-promotional use. For details write to Special Sales Manager at Motorbooks International Wholesalers & Distributors, Galtier Plaza, Suite 200, 380 Jackson Street, St. Paul, MN 55101-3885 USA.

Library of Congress Cataloging-in-Publication Data Available

ISBN 0-7603-1079-3

On the front cover: The Farmall Cub replaced the Farmall 100 and was intended to be the perfect tractor for small farms. *Andy Kraushaar*

Frontispiece: The Cub Cadet was a favorite of business owners as well as homeowners and was useful in all seasons.

On the title page: A 1959–1963 styled Cub Lo-Boy, outfitted with turf tread tires and a sickle bar mower.

On the back cover: Even the largest yards were mowed quickly with the IH Cub Cadet 1X8 or 1X9 series.

Designed by Dan Perry

Printed in Hong Kong

CONTENTS

PREFACE

The Farmall X tractor or Cub, as we know it, was the last major mechanical breakthrough to eliminate the horse and mule from the farm. This small one-plow tractor was specifically designed for the farm of this size. With the onset of World War II, the Cub was delayed in its market entry, which may have limited some of its sales potential. The farm labor shortages caused by the war would not have been avoided in the United States, but the Cub may have helped ease them.

The direct descendent of the Cub, the Cub Lo-Boy, opened a new market of tractor sales that International Harvester (IH) desperately wanted to penetrate: The industrial/commercial market. This adapted tractor opened new sales avenues for IH and helped spark new life into the Cub tractor market sales. Through several body style changes, the Cub evolved with the changing world; often just having a sheet metal update to match the other new IH tractors of the day.

I am sure that IH engineers never envisioned that the Cub and its descendent, the Cub Lo-Boy, would have the production life span that they did. The adaptation of the Cub transmission and differential assembly to form the Cub Cadet tractor only helped to bolster the reputation of these great little tractors. Tens of thousands of all three tractors can be found on the farms, factories, fairways, and garages across America today and in many other parts of the world.

The newly instituted laws governing vehicle emissions, and the fact that the Cub tooling and its factory were both badly in need of an overhaul, helped lead to the demise of the Cub. The modern compact tractors that are so wildly popular today all owe their existence to the *first* compact tractor, the one that set the bar of excellence: the Farmall Cub.

To put every detail of the Cub, Cub Lo-Boy, and Cub Cadet in a single volume is not possible. However, I hope that this book helps to expand a few of the stories and ideas that IH had when it made these great little tractors.

ACKNOWLEDGMENTS

Thank you, once again, to the friendly staff of the State Historical Society of Wisconsin and especially employees Guy Fay and Lee Grady. These two individuals have been charged with the gargantuan job of safekeeping and inventorying the IH/McCormick collection at the state archives. Finding boxes of sales literature, photos, and production data for me that quickly made this book research go much easier. I thank you both.

Thanks to my grandparents Harvey and Alice Kilian. My exposure to IH in my early childhood was often spent driving their H or M Farmalls in the machine shed with my cousin, Doug. They helped get me hooked on IH.

A special note of thanks to my parents, Ed and Cathy, who never minded my collection of IH toy tractors, which greatly expanded from three tractors to nearly 1,000, even if it did take up a lot of their basement space. I finally convinced my dad to buy a Cub Cadet to mow his five-acre yard; even he admits it was the best machine he ever bought. I think he really likes the 24-7 parts and service I give him instead.

Thanks to the staff at Carter & Gruenewald Co. Inc., of Brooklyn and Juda, Wisconsin; they were extra flexible with me. Their Web site, www.cngco.com, is a valuable Cub and Cub Cadet resource. Their cooperation, in my research and fact-finding, was exceptional, and the experiences I have working there are incredible.

My thanks also extend to Jeff Powell for his expert research. Thanks to Jim Becker for the outstanding clues on Cub production and features. The FAQ he maintains at www.atis.net is invaluable.

Thanks to the great folks at www.ihcubcadet.com. They were the source of inspiration for this entire project. To produce a book with ideas and input from them is a real joy. Even though this project was delayed for couple years, I hope it was worth the wait. I'm sure that readers will always want *more*, but that is what sequels are for.

I must say thanks to MBI Publishing. The project was shelved awhile, but finally it got back on its rails. Thanks for all of the help.

Thank you, finally, to my wife, Charlene. She may have thought that the photos I have collected would never get used (or even get put away), but here they are. She never doubts my ideas and activities when I go on a tractor "safari", even if they are sometimes unbelievable.

CHAPTER 1

THE CUB TRACTOR IS BORN

International Harvester's (IH) marketing department recognized that there was a tractor-marketing segment not being addressed by manufactures. The rapid mechanization of farms, and the transformation of the landscape of the United States from a mostly agrarian nation to an industrial and urban nation were cause for change.

IH recognized that a tractor market existed for the part time or urban farmer and also the small rural farmer. The farmer who owned a single horse or mule also needed a tractor. The tractors being manufactured in the 1920s and 1930s were too big and clumsy to fit into small compact fields, and to work in closely cultivated crops without damaging them. IH devised a plan to build such a tractor for these customers. It was code-named Farmall X by IH's engineering department, or the "baby Farmall" as others in the company knew it.

After the planting is done, the Cub has a mid-mounted cultivator attached and heads to the fields to attack weeds. Because of the Cub's unique offset seating design, the operator has a clear view of the work ahead. *State Historical Society of Wisconsin*

The tractor that started it all. The Farmall Cub, serial number 501, was the first Cub built. International Harvester would continue to build the Cub (in slightly modified forms) the next 30 years. This would be the longest production run of any IH tractor. Today, Cub 501 is safely stored in a private collection. *State Historical Society of Wisconsin*

While most tractor companies focused only on bigger and more powerful tractors, IH didn't forget about the "little guy." The Farmall X was the answer for these potential tractor-buying customers. On December 20, 1944 IH's tractor and implement engineering divisions showed the first prototypes of the Farmall X to IH management. None of the parts used to make the Farmall X came from either the Farmall A or Farmall B, which meant there would be some expensive tooling

before tractor production and profits could be made.

IH built smaller tractors in the 1930s aimed at reaching the "horse drawn" farmer. The Farmall F-12, F-14, and the Cultivision A, and AV were scaled down versions of their bigger brothers. The new models met the needs of the farmer who farmed 50 to 85 acres, but were still at a price level too high for the 40-acres-or-less farmer.

IH needed a smaller tractor to reach this untapped market. The Farmall X (later renamed the Farmall Cub) was

the tractor to reach these farmers. IH intended to market the Farmall X in the $400 range, therefore, its net manufacturing cost had to be around $225. To achieve this price target it was proposed to use a 2-cylinder upright engine. However, the smoothness of a 4-cylinder engine and its torque characteristics were chosen instead.

The Farmall Cub tractor was essentially a two-third scale version of the Farmall Super A tractor. Farmall engineers and marketers envisioned the Cub as the gasoline tractor

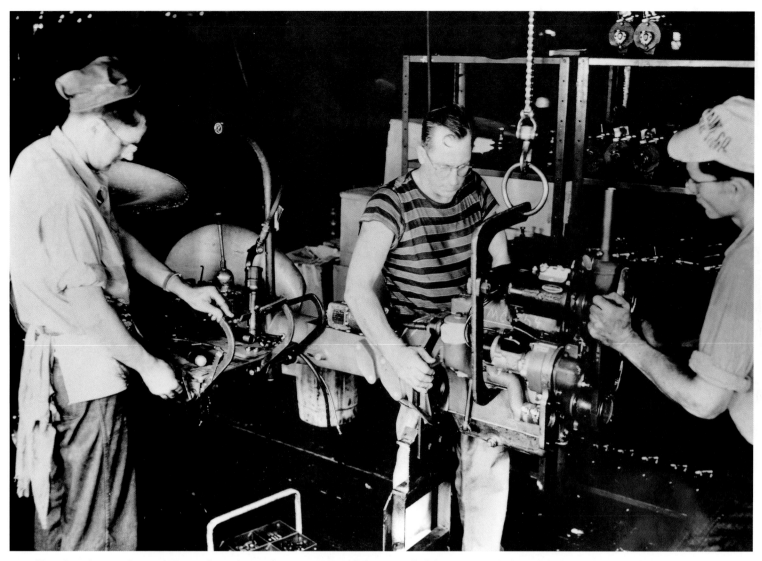

Assembling the Cub, IH workers at the Louisville Works join the C-60 engine with the rear half of the tractor; the brake pedals also are being installed. Notice the large rack of black-painted generator/relay assemblies on the shelves in the background. *State Historical Society of Wisconsin*

replacement for the one horse or mule farmer in America. The post–World War II era brought forth a new wave of farmers: Folks who had a small urban acreage or large vegetable gardens. Tobacco growers also were targeted as a prolific buyer of Cub tractors.

Little did IH management know that the Cub and its descendents (Cub Lo-Boys, and Cub Cadets) would become wildly popular tractors, and affix themselves as icons of American Farming and the growing trend of urbanization. They had the notoriety

of being the longest production run of any single-model IH tractor. The Cub was built from 1947 to 1979, a span of 32 years that saw not only the landscape of farming change, but also saw the IH company change. It is ironic that Cub did not have the largest production volume ever; both the Farmall H and Farmall M outsold the Cub and its descendents.

The company's engineering plan for the Cub was well under way before World War II. During the war years, IH devoted nearly all of its

resources to the output of machines, tools, and weapons, which played a huge role in winning the war. The Cub was delayed to keep the American war machine running. Whenever possible, IH engineers did sneak some "Cub time" into their schedule to keep the progress made thus far, alive. At the end of World War II, IH launched an all out war of its own. The war was to get the Cub from blueprint drawings, into a working tractor. The company's post-war product expansion program cost $150 million. More than

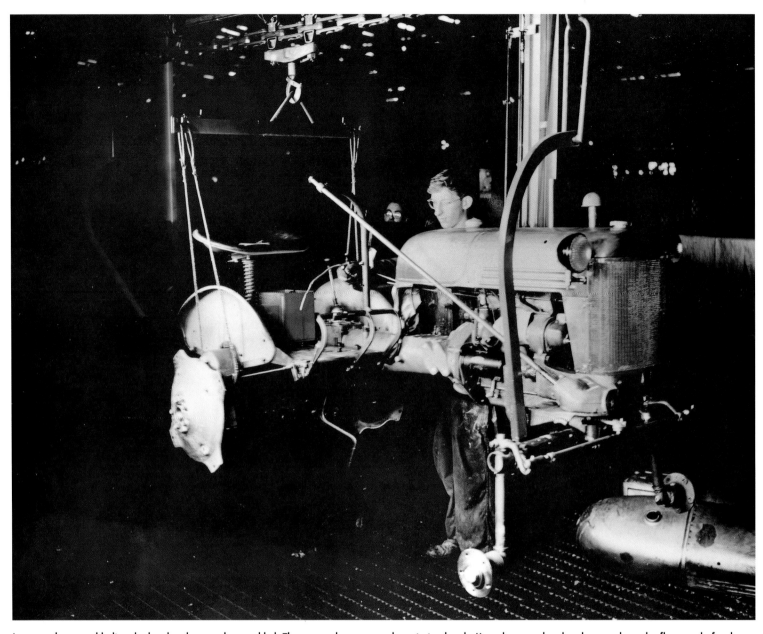

Later on the assembly line the hood and gas tank are added. The tractor then goes to the painting booth. Note the extra hood and gas tank on the floor ready for the next Cub on the line. The starter and headlights are painted black then they will be repainted with IH 50 red in the painting booth. *State Historical Society of Wisconsin*

one-third of that amount was spent on the Cub. IH hoped the Cub would extend the benefits of small-tractor farming power to a vast market never before served by tractor manufacturers. The company recognized the enormous possibilities for business represented by the buying power alone of the small-farm owners. To tap into this market could bring IH untold millions of dollars of revenue,

increased market share, owner loyalty, and more profitable dealers.

The Farmall Cub was produced at the Louisville Works, with IH's long-established policies in mind. First, to design and build in large quantities the kind of equipment needed by its end users; second, to sell these machines at prices which will permit the widest possible use; and third, to market these tractors in

such volumes as to generate large profits for IH.

IH announced the Cub tractor to the public at its late 1945 summer field demonstration program held at the Harvester Farm in Hinsdale, IL. IH heavily promoted the Cub well in advance of its release, even though it would take IH another two years to actually produce the tractor for public sale. This media frenzy not only

After painting the Cub, decals and tires are attached.The Cub is nearly completed and soon will be on a railroad flat car or truck to one of the many IH dealers in the United States. Under the cabinet used to store the tractors decals are extra tires and mufflers awaiting installation on other units. Note that the decal on the battery box is not perfectly straight. Because of the mass number of Cub tractors made and assembly time limits, not every decal was perfectly centered; it's very common to find misplaced decals on Cub tractors. *State Historical Society of Wisconsin*

increased buying, it also helped IH convey to the marketplace that it intended to make machines for every farm, regardless acreage.

When International finally introduced the Farmall Cub to the public in 1947, it culminated the $55 million the company had spent for the research, engineering and machine tooling it to

take this tractor into production. This expenditure was a tremendous amount of money in a post-war era. IH had planned to introduce the Cub several years earlier, but the war prevented this from happening. During the World War II years there was a large-scale trend toward larger, commercially operated farms. IH recognized the

value of keeping the family farm economically sound as one of its corporate goals. By offering the small, low-priced tractor with specially designed implements to match, IH hoped to reverse that trend. This trend of growing numbers of smaller farms never happened, in fact IH was soon joined by other tractor manufacturers

Equiped with a one-bottom moldboard plow, the Farmall Cub didn't set any plowing records, but its targeted market audience didn't farm by the section. Even though the tractor had only 9 horsepower, the gearing in the Cub helped to make this tractor a powerhouse in the field. *State Historical Society of Wisconsin*

in a race of ever-increasing tractor horsepower and size.

As a businessman, the farmer had to be profitable to stay in business, and the low-priced Cub tractor was an important tool that allowed the small-acreage farmer to do so. IH chairman of the board, Fowler McCormick stated in 1937 that International Harvester was to be put on the record as believing in the preservation and future of the family size farm.

IH's main competitor to the Cub was the Allis-Chalmers model G. The G was marketed more as a garden tractor than a farm tractor. It had a rear-mounted engine/transmission and only accepted mid-mounted implements. With 10 horsepower on the belt, the G was nearly identical in power to the Cub, except the Cub could accept either front-, mid- or rear-mounted implements. Both tractors offered unique version of Culti-vision, a term coined by IH. Allis built the G from 1948 to 1955, roughly the same time period as the original mesh grille Cub.

IH used its own 4-cylinder, thermosyphon-cooled, gasoline-powered engine in the Cub. This engine was of a bore-in-block design, meaning that the engine does not have replaceable sleeves or wear liners.

A 2 5/8 inch bore by 2 3/4 inch stroke yielded a 59.5 cubic inch displacement. The engine was called the C-60, C representing carburetor and 60 the cubic inch displacement of the engine. IH used this engine-identifying method on all of its engines. The C-60 engine was of an L head-type design, meaning that the valves were not located above the pistons but in a pocket area beside the combustion chamber. Only the spark plug was located above the piston.

One feature commonly found on other tractors made during the pre and post-World War II years was the choice of fuel used to power the

A two-row trailing planter was ideally matched to the Cub. This tractor is applying fertilizer from the large hopper mounted on the tractor. Note the vertical steel rod at the front of the Cub that acts as a steering sight. *State Historical Society of Wisconsin*

tractor. IH offered diesel-, gasoline- and kerosene- (distillate) powered tractors in a wide variety of models and horsepower ranges. The Farmall Cub was only offered as a gasoline-powered version. The Cub could run on kerosene but it lacked the gasoline starting tank and radiator shutter attachment commonly associated with this fuel type. A clear glass sediment bowl under the fuel tank not only filtered out water and other impurities, but with a simple glance, the operator could check to see if the system was dirty. The fuel system used a gravity-fed, 3/4-inch, updraft International carburetor. A secondary screen at the carburetor's fuel inlet trapped any dirt that the sediment filter may have missed. The company designed a Magneto ignition specifically for the Cub. The J4 magneto was standard equipment on Cubs. IH offered its own distributor ignition as optional equipment. The distributor was considered standard equipment when the battery ignition package was ordered. All of the distributors IH used on the Cub were similar to those used on its larger farm tractors. The main difference was that the distributor drive shaft had a different timing advance built into the shaft. These distributors have an automatic spark-advance feature. This package offered battery-powered starting, two headlamps, one rear work lamp, and distributor ignition. Starting was accomplished through a bendix-drive 6-volt starter made by the Delco Remy Company. This starter engaged a metal-toothed ring gear on the Cub engine flywheel. The starter was located on the right side of the tractor directly below the oil filter housing. Electric starting and lighting became a standard feature in 1958.

The C-60 engine was unique in that it had an oil-filter housing cast into the engine block. Only the filter lid was removed to service the

IH worked hard to promote the Cub to everyone, and even women were a targeted marketing group. Many of the potential buyers were small-farm families with the "lady of the farm" having a greater influence on purchasing. IH was eager to ask women to try the Cub to see if they liked it. *State Historical Society of Wisconsin*

cartridge-type oil filter. This cartridge-type filter could trap dirt particles as small as .000039 inch. The Cub was first equipped with a Purolator-brand umbrella-style filter. In the Cub's later production life (1960s) this umbrella-style would be changed to a true canister-style filter. The canister-style filters offered a larger filtering surface area to clean the engine oil more efficiently. A spin-on-style filter was never offered in the more than 30

year production of the Cub. The oil pressure gauge screwed directly into the filter housing. The engine was filled with fresh oil through a tube located on the left side of the engine. When the breather cap was removed from the tube, the attached oil-level bayonet or dipstick showed the current level of oil in the engine. It is important to check the engine oil level every time before the tractor is started. If the level is low, add

sufficient oil to bring the level into the safe range indicated on the stick.

Vital pressure lubrication of the engine was accomplished through the use of an engine-driven oil pump located in the center of the engine. A floating oil-pickup screen in the oil-pan sump fed the pump. After going through the oil pump, the oil is forced through drilled passages to the crankshaft bearings, the connecting rod bearings, and the camshaft bearings.

Here is a rather odd photo showing a Cub powering a belt-driven electric generator. The drive belt is under the large boxed shield. A high clearance Cub appears in the background. This photo appears to have been taken at an IH dealer display. *State Historical Society of Wisconsin*

All of the critical engine-bearing surfaces are protected continually and positively with a light film of friction-reducing oil.

The Cub had an oil capacity of 3 quarts. IH recommended that the engine oil and filter element be replaced every 120 working hours of operation. This author recommends that the engine oil be changed every 100 hours of operation, and that only straight 30-weight (10-weight in colder climates or during winter use) Lo-Ash oil made by IH, now Case New Holland (CNH) is used. The Lo-Ash oil from CNH has a lower, s ulfated-ash content than other oils. This lower ash content can reduce valve deposits and torching, resulting in a cleaner-burning engine.

When the original Cub owners' manual was printed, it suggested using a 30-weight *non-detergent*-type lubricating oil in the engine. This may have been a state of the art lubricant in the 1940s, oils today are vastly improved and every engine should be treated with them. Many times, Cubs are bought used or secondhand and the oil type is unknown. An easy way to see if your Cub engine has detergent or non-detergent oil is to remove the engine oil pan or the side cover to access the valve tappets. If large accumulations of sludge are present, the tractor probably

has non-detergent oil flowing through its engine. If the areas are clean, detergent oil has been used. Because detergent oil holds the dirt particle in suspension until they are filtered out this is logically the better choice. Changing a non-detergent engine to detergent oil can require multiple filter and oil flushing. The detergent oils will loosen the deposits inside the engine and eventually move them to the filter.

Running at a rated speed of 1,600 rpm, the C-60 produced a "whopping" 9.25 horsepower on the belt, and 8 horsepower at the drawbar. This was no H or M tractor, it was a lil' one. International built the C-60 engine in house on a separate assembly line at the Louisville production plant, using the latest design technology of the time. Thousands of hours were spent on engineering, design, research, and testing this engine. The C-60 was state of the art when it was introduced and its basic design remained virtually unchanged in its more than 30-year production life span. The area that was re-engineered was the crankshaft and pistons. The original Cub offered cast-iron flat-top pistons. In the late 1960s, IH changed these to cast-aluminum domed-top pistons. These pistons helped the C-60 engine jump from 10 horsepower to 15 horsepower and eventually to 18 horsepower. When the C-60 engine was outfitted with aluminum-domed pistons, the engine compression ratio soared from 6.5:1 to 7.5:1.

Company engineers also made modifications to the camshaft for added durability at higher-rated engine speeds. The camshaft is a single-piece drop-forged shaft with three bearing journals machined into bores in the engine crankcase; valve tappets were also improved with the new cam. The Cub crankshaft was drop-forged, high-carbon steel, statically and dynamically balanced; bearing journals were induction hardened. The connecting rods were a heat-treated I-beam-type design for maximum strength. IH offered a high-altitude cylinder head as optional equipment, along with exhaust-valve rotators for the Cub engine.

To control engine speed, IH engineers outfitted the C-60 engine with a simple fly-ball, variable-speed-type governor. The governor depends on centrifugal force made by weights that rotate on a shaft. These weights are counteracted by a variable-tensioned spring. As the weights move, they also control the movement of a connecting linkage that controls the throttle opening in the carburetor. When the tractor is started and the operator advances the engine speed lever forward, the governor weights move outward by centrifugal force until the governor spring counteracts their movement. A weak spring (very common with use and age in any tractor) will produce less resistance, and the engines performance will be noticeably slower, sometimes non-responsive (broken springs are characteristic of this).

As the governor spring stabilizes the air-fuel mixture of the carburetor, the mixture will be sufficiently regulated by the throttle-shaft valve to maintain the engine speed.

This Farmall Cub has skeleton rear wheels, and the front axle is set extra wide. This might be an indicator that the mounted planter is planting a bedded- or mound-grown crop. A Cub with this unique wheel setup can be very hard to find today. *State Historical Society of Wisconsin*

A center-mounted earth-grading blade can help you to grade over high spots in the field or to build terraces. The rear wheel weights not only aid in traction, but also in tractor stability. Notice the driver's pith helmet; IH dealers offered these unique caps in several colors to farmers in the 1950s. *State Historical Society of Wisconsin*

The operator controls the engine speed by moving a single lever, which increases or decreases tension on the spring, not by a direct connection to the carburetor throttle valve. By increasing the spring tension, the weights move inward, which in turn opens the throttle-shaft valve, further increasing engine speed until the spring equalizes the force of the weights. To slow an engine down, this mechanical process is reversed. The linkage between the governor and the carburetor is adjustable to achieve full power at engine-rated rpm.

The governor drive gears also act as the ignition-unit drive. The governor drive gears are marked for proper mesh with their mating gears at top dead center of the number one cylinder on its compression stroke. If the governor is removed, be sure to time the engine to this position first.

The Cub's engine-cooling system was a copy of that used by its big brothers, the Farmalls A and B. All three feature a cooling system that uses the thermosyphon principle to cool the engine. Coolant (either water or antifreeze) circulates through the engine and radiator by thermosyphon or heat-moving action. As water heats up, it will move or expand. Steam locomotives are prime examples of this because they use highly pressurized water. As the coolant gets hot, it expands and enters the top tank of the radiator. The cold air blast from the cooling fan cools the liquid causing it to settle to the bottom of the radiator, and then flow back to the engine block to replace the heated coolant.

This explains why Cubs and Cub Lo-Boys do not have engine water pumps. The radiator was built as a flat tube design that was protected by the grille and bolted to the steering-gear housing base. A gasket sealed the connection between this housing and the radiator. A fan shroud on the radiator greatly increased the engine fan's efficiency, thereby reducing the chance of overheating.

It is imperative that the radiator be checked daily, not only for coolant level, but for cleanliness. If the fins become bent they can be carefully straightened with a radiator brush. If the radiator is clogged, remove and take it to an IH dealer for service. The use of radiator stop leaks is not recommended because they highly reduce the efficiency of the radiator to transfer heat. IH also recommended that the coolant be changed twice a year. A handy drain plug is located at the bottom of the front steering housing to accomplish this. When refilling the radiator, the coolant level should be brought to the bottom of the filler neck. If the coolant level is higher, the system will find its own level when the tractor is operated by boiling out an excess.

The Farmall Cub featured a simple three-forward, one-speed reverse transmission with a bull gear/pinion final

Years before the zero-turn mowers became popular, IH offered its Farmall Cub with an optional front-mounted gang reel mower. The single hydraulic lift control made raising the mower effortless. Getting close to trees or other objects was easy with this Cub. *State Historical Society of Wisconsin*

drive. The transmission speeds in the Cub were ideally matched for every crop and condition. First gear was 2 mph, second gear 3 mph, and third gear 6 mph; reverse speed was 2.7 mph. The transmission was built using sliding spur cut gears. The transmission was not synchronized, meaning that down-shifting on-the-go was not possible without loud, and sometimes violent, gear clashing. A foot-operated clutch

controlled the transmission of engine power, not only to the driving wheels, but also to the rear PTO/belt pulley (if equipped). This clutch was built as a single disc/single stage-type clutch. The standard equipment clutch an Auburn brand; a Rockford brand was an optional, heavy-duty replacement.

A pressed, carbon-fiber bearing was used as the release bearing in the Cub. A true roller bearing (like those

on larger IH tractors) would never be outfitted on the Cub. This stationary release bearing would engage the drive-clutch release levers (sometimes called fingers) to disengage the engine drive clutch. An operator who would ride the clutch would partially depress the clutch pedal all of the time. This not only rapidly wore out the release bearing, it did not allow the clutch pressure plate to fully engage the

While most people associate the Cub with agricultural crops, tree farming can also showcase the Cub's talents. Here a young man is cultivating Christmas trees with a Cub. The high ground clearance made the Cub ideally suited for this. *State Historical Society of Wisconsin*

driving disc, allowing the disc to slip. This slippage caused tremendous heat to be generated, often times warping the disc or getting the pressure plate hot enough to melt the disc lining. When you smell burnt clutch while driving, you are either riding the clutch, or it is in dire need of replacement or an adjustment.

The use of a variable-speed engine governor allowed the operator to get those in between speeds for varying crop conditions. The transmission used the latest design of spring-loaded rawhide oil seals, that kept dirt and dust out. When overhauling a Cub transmission it is not uncommon to find that replacement seals are

sometimes one half of the thickness of the original seals. Vast improvements in sealing material technology have made these parts very compact in thickness. This author highly recommends that when a situation like the above occurs, two seals should be installed. While this may add to the net cost of the repair, if a single seal is

Here is the view from the operator's seat on the Famall Cub tractor. Note the clear, unobstructed view to the front and directly below. This feature was termed Cultivision by IH and was a major selling feature. By having the operator's seat offset from the tractor centerline, damage to delicate plants could be avoided. *State Historical Society of Wisconsin*

installed and it happens to rest exactly where the old seal did, it probably has worn, and there is slight groove in the shaft. Oil will leak past the seal as if nothing were installed at all.

IH used over 23 ball and roller bearings in the Cub to keep friction to a minimum and assure smooth power transmission from the engine to the draw bar. Two distinct shifting levers are used on the Cub and Cub Lo-Boy. The straight lever is for use on all Cubs without a deluxe cushion seat (this has a pipe frame with a small backrest and square seat cushion). An angled lever was used on all of the Cub Lo-Boys and on the Cubs with deluxe seat. The angle lever shifter was also used on all gear-drive Cub Cadets. The Cub transmission is filled with 80-90-gear oil lubricant.

The use of large, bull-pinion final-drive gears encased in separate gear housings allowed the Cub to have more than 20 3/8 inches of crop clearance and minimized crop damage. This was vital when cultivating high-value

A single-row planter with fertilizer attachment is being used on this bright summer day. The silver hopper holds fertilizer, the blue painted hopper holds the plant seeds. Both are injected into the ground at precise depths for maximum plant vigor. *State Historical Society of Wisconsin*

vegetable crops. The gears in these housings have induction hardened teeth and ride on tapered roller bearings to take the heaviest punishment of tasks. A precision, automotive-style differential with spiral bevel ring and pinion gears was constantly bated in oil and was designed to handle large-torque shock loads. Adjustable-tread wheel rims mounted on stamped steel wheels allowed wheel tread settings from 40 to 56 inches wide. A set of

special 5-inch axle spacers was optional for wider wheel-tread applications.

The Cub non-adjustable tread with front axle as standard equipment; an adjustable tread axle was optional. This adjustable axle sold for an extra $12 in 1950. To adjust the tread width, the operator moved a pin and bolted a clamping block in various holes in the front axle tube. These holes allowed the front wheel spacing to be adjusted in 4-inch

increments from 40 5/8 to 56 5/8 inches wide. IH offered cast iron weights in 26 pounds to fit the front wheels and in 145 pounds for the rear wheels. Both styles of weights were bolted to the wheel disc with two bolts, and additional weights could be stack-bolted to optimize tractor ballasting requirements. The front wheel weights were also used as the rear wheel weights on the Cub Cadet garden tractors. Today these

This Farmall Cub is cultivating a nice field of check-row planted corn. Crops planted with a check-row planter could be cultivated at 90-degree angles to ensure complete weed removal. This once-common farming practice is now just a memory of the past. *State Historical Society of Wisconsin*

cast weights can be scarce to find and are highly sought after by collectors.

A popular optional feature that was sold by IH dealers was the Touch Control hydraulic lifting system. This was a scaled-down version of those found on the Super A or Farmall C.

The first Cubs built did not offer the Touch Control as factory-installed because the system was not yet perfected. Subsequently, IH machined the castings to allow its dealers to add the Touch Control system if the customer chose. The major difference was that the Cub has a single control lever, single rockshaft and single hydraulic cylinder. The Touch Control system offers two-way control of mounted implements. This was especially handy to put down pressure on front-, center-, or rear-mounted grading blades. An adjustable indicator on the Touch Control lever quadrant is handy to use when a uniform implement working depth is required. The Touch Control unit mounts directly behind the engine under the gas tank. It looks like a large block with rotating lever arms on each side. A rear-mounted rockshaft can be added to tractors whose implements require it.

With Touch Control hydraulics, the operator can effortlessly lift heavy implements with the touch of a finger. An engine-driven hydraulic pump located on the left side of the engine powered the Touch Control unit. Because it was driven by the timing gears on the engine, this pump ran when the engine did. A mesh screen inside the Touch Control block acted as the filter for the system. The Touch Control unit was fully self-contained with its own lubricant called Touch Control Fluid. This oil has been greatly refined over the years and now is know as Hy-Tran Ultra. While this Touch Control hydraulic lift was used exclusively for implements when first installed on the Cub, it would later be the lifting power source for the rear hitching system called the Fast Hitch.

The list price of a Farmall Cub with standard equipment was $545 F.O.B. Louisville Works in 1947.

Many of IH's other factories produced component parts for the Cub. Tractor Works in Chicago; West Pullman Works in West Pulman, Illinois; and Milwaukee Works in Milwaukee, Wisconsin, furnished forgings. The engine governor weights and raw carburetor castings were made at Tractor Works; transmission differential shafts, reverse first, second, and third speed gears and clutch shafts came from Milwaukee Works; and West Pullman Works made the rear axles, magnetos, and completed carburetors. West Pullman also was the source of the Cub's screws, bolts, rivet and roller bearings. The Rock Falls Works in Rock Falls, Illinois, furnished some clips, control rods, and coiled steel springs. The Grey Iron Foundry at the Indianapolis Works Indianapolis, Indiana, made castings for the Cub cylinder heads, pistons, flywheels, crankcases, differential cases, rear-axle housings, steering-gear housings, and transmission cases. The McCormick Works in Chicago was the source of the Cub steering-gear housing bases

and many malleable iron castings. IH's Canton Works in Canton, Illinois, and Rock Falls Works both made scaled down implements to be used with the tractor that "worked like a bear, but was a Cub in size."

Over 14 million pounds of steel was used from IH's Wisconsin Steel Mills to produce Cub hoods, fenders, steering shafts, axles, etc. for the initial production run of the Cub tractor. This was a big undertaking by IH's many component parts factories to get the Cub off the line and in the field.

The first production Cub (serial number 501) was set on the assembly line at Louisville Works to start its journey into history on Saturday afternoon May 10, 1947. By the end of Monday the 12th, the Cub was barely halfway down the assembly line. Tuesday brought more progress to the pilot run or assembly test model as it started to look like a tractor. At 1:50 p.m. 501 was out of the paint booth and drying. It reached its assembly culmination, the end of the line at 2:40 p.m. Louisville Works Manager J. E. Harris boarded the first Cub and at 3:05 p.m., let the clutch out and started the engine. This also marked the start of the longest production run of a single model tractor in the company's history.

IH sent number 501 to the Canton Works for test fitting of the many implements that were to be offered with Cub. The next five Cubs, serial numbers 502, 503, 504, 505, and 506 were outfitted with Spanish language decals and sent to the IH Works in Salitillo, Mexico. Farmall Cub serial number 501 was eventually sold to a farmer in Wisconsin. This farmer also purchased nearly every single Cub implement available at the time for use on his produce farm. Only recently

was this Cub restored to its original condition. The locations of Cubs 502 through 506 are currently unknown to this author, they are believed to have been scrapped.

Building a Factory for the Cub

The company expected that the majority of the Cubs made would be sold for tobacco farming. While looking at possible factory sites to build the Cub, IH concentrated its efforts on a site near the tobacco belt in the United States. This geographical area comprised the states of Kentucky, Tennessee, and the Carolina's. With World War II still firmly gripping nearly every country around the globe in battles, International Harvester was planning to build the Farmall Cub tractor as soon as the war ended. A new factory located in Wood River, IL, was selected to be the home of Farmall Cub tractor production. Land procurement and site grading started in 1945. In 1946, IH dropped its plans for this factory and announced it had purchased the former Curtis Aircraft Company factory in Louisville KY, from the War Assets Administration. This would become known as the Louisville Works or as most IH enthusiast calls it "Louisville". International promised the townspeople of Wood River that eventually an IH factory would be built there, but it never materialized. The exact reason to switch at the last minute to buy Louisville has not yet been discovered, but the lack of post-war materials, and the fact that the Curtis factory may have been "too good of a deal to pass up" are the strongest theories at this time.

The first IH tractor built at Louisville was shipped on April 11, 1947 after extensive re-tooling and

The snow must be moved! At the Wayne, IL, railroad depot, a Farmall Cub with a front-mounted blade quickly clears snow from the station platform. The daily express is due in and with it will be mail and other cargo that needs to be handled. *State Historical Society of Wisconsin*

remodeling of the factory for tractor production. Only one month later the first Cub finally rolled down the assembly line. The Farmall Cub, Super A and new row-crop tractor Farmall C were all produced at Louisville when it opened.

Louisville Works was a complete manufacturing facility. It took in rough stock and produced finished product. The plant had its own foundry that produced many hundreds of different gray iron castings, not only for its own production, but for other IH factories too. The foundry had an iron melt capacity of almost 1,000 tons a day and was IH's largest.

A modern forge shop with 14 presses ranging in size from 1,000 tons to 8,000 tons produced, engine crankshafts, gear blanks and other forgings for many IH factories. An engine assembly line produced a dozen different basic models of 4- and 6-cylinder gasoline engines for IH and other companies. The six tractor assembly lines at Louisville produced not only the Cub, Cub Lo-Boy, and Cub Cadet, but small- and mid-size agricultural tractors, forklifts and the company's line of industrial wheeled tractors. The plant area included more than 145 acres, with 48 acres under roof.

In the three years of operating Louisville Works from 1946 to 1949, IH incurred a total operating loss of over $21.5 million. Delays in tooling the Cub sent parts vendors' schedules into a spiral. By the time Louisville was ready to make tractors, the parts vendors had committed to other customers. The large union labor force at Louisville (just as at most other IH factories) severely limited the company's management's choices on what to do. As parts shortages became clear, only partial assembly of units could be accomplished until the missing pieces arrived.

CHAPTER 2

WHITE DEMOS AND LO-BOYS

The 1950s would see International Harvester (IH) expand the Cub tractor line with a new low slung model called the Lo-Boy. The Cub Lo-Boy was introduced to meet the growing demand in the industrial and commercial markets. New advancements in hydraulics and basic styling changes would dominate the Cub line in the 1950s. IH built four differently styled Cubs in the 1950s more than at any other time in the tractor's history. After an initial surge in sales, the Cub sales tapered off. IH had several programs to help bolster sagging sales and retain or grow market share. The mid-century White Demo Tractor Program was one of these programs. At IH, it was time to make tractors and get Cubs out into the hands of potential users.

A center-mounted gang-reel mower and a Farmall Cub help keep any farmstead or estate in perfect condition. The gutsy C-60 engine in the Cub was ideally matched to jobs such as this. The hydraulic attachment lift made operation of the implements seem effortless. *State Historical Society of Wisconsin*

This rare photo of a 1950 IH White Demo Cub with a hydraulic front-end loader gives a good look at the white tractor. The front loader put a large amount of stress on the front axle and spindles. Notice the large cast-iron wheel weights on the rear tractor wheels. The White Demonstrator Cub was built only in early 1950. These are fast becoming highly collectible tractors. *State Historical Society of Wisconsin*

Mid-Century Program IH White Demo Cubs

To celebrate the mid–20th century mark (1950), IH decided to get aggressive with special tractor demonstration programs. IH used specially painted white tractors to draw the attention of potential customers. Only the Farmall Super A, Farmall C and Farmall Cub are believed to be the true White Demonstrator tractors that IH offered as factory-built models. White Demo. It is believed that the White Demos were built only in the months of January, February, and March of 1950.

It is relatively easy to identify if you have a true White Demo. One characteristic marking is the casting of the letter L on the clutch-tube housing. This is typically found in an upside down position to the rest of the numbers, with the letters cast into the part.

Another method to determine if you have a White Demo is to scratch the underside of the hood, or other inconspicuous area that is commonly missed during repainting. When the White Demo tractors were repainted to IH red, very few were completely disassembled. Therefore, it can be relatively easy to find clues to find a White Demo.

The most obvious method of verifying a true White Demo is to compare the serial number. Farmall Cubs from serial number 99356 to 106516

Who says the Cub was limited to just farmchores? Here a Cub tows a twin engine airplane. Cub sales to airlines probably increased ten-fold after this photo was taken, but the Cub was never offered as a special tarmac version. The uses for a Cub truly were endless. *State Historical Society of Wisconsin*

are believed to be white-painted demonstrator Cubs that IH built. After the Mid Century program ended, IH expected its dealers to repaint the white Cubs back to standard IH red before they were sold.

IH used an aggressive marketing program to spur demonstrations and, hopefully, sales of IH tractors and machinery. IH encouraged its dealer network to out-work, out-sell, and out-demonstrate the IH line to not only

loyal IH customers, but to those who had competitive tractors or who were new to the marketplace. Large field demonstrations that had a county fair look to them were held nationwide in the spring and summer months of 1950. To get the attention of potential customers, dealers used colorful tents, tractor parades, and decorative bunting. The company even used a creative marketing scheme showing Boy Scout of America troops using Cub tractors.

When the Cub was first introduced in 1947, sales skyrocketed for the first two years, then they leveled off and even started to decline. IH marketing was quick to recognize this trend and launched a massive tractor demonstration program that would not only mark the middle of the 20th century, but also IH's dominance in the market place since its formation in 1902. IH hoped that the sales volume of the Cub and the other

Summer is not the only season for Cubs. The cold winter affords snowplowing duties that the Cub can handle with ease. The spring-trip, front-mounted blade would tip over if an obstruction was hit. *State Historical Society of Wisconsin*

tractors built at Louisville would rebound.

Very few, if any, original White Demo tractors exist today. Many restored versions can be seen at various tractor shows/rallies. Some are accurately restored, others are just painted white, many times incorrectly. A few fake White Demos have been made. If you are contemplating the purchase or investigating the

authenticity of a White Demo Cub, follow the guidelines given above. The tractor serial number is the first place to start checking.

IH encouraged its dealers to not only demonstrate, but more importantly, sell the Cub *system* of farming to farmers. Some dealers even assigned their salesman to tractor demo routes where they would stop by every prospective customer. If they

didn't sell a Cub or other IH tractor, they could try to sell an implement, truck, or IH refrigerator. Not only was the tractor heavily marketed, more importantly the Cub implements were emphasized to prospective customers. It was felt that the only way to achieve the full effect of the Cub tractor was to use the specially matched Cub implements. By doing so, the farmer could be assured that the implement he

Drilling holes with an earth auger was never easier when you had a power auger mounted on the Cub. If you needed a few fence post holes or some tree plantings on the farmstead, this was definitely the best way to do it. *State Historical Society of Wisconsin*

bought was sized right for the Cub. Not to big, not to small.

Basic Farmall Cub Equipment and Prices

A standard issue Farmall Cub came equipped as follows in 1950: 4-cylinder C-60 engine, vertically adjustable drawbar, adjustable rear wheel tread, fenders, foot operated differential steering brakes, three speed transmission, magneto ignition, non-adjustable front axle, spring-mounted implement-style seat, 3.00-12 inch two ply front tires, and 6-24 inch two ply rear tires. The base price of the standard Farmall Cub was $659.

A list of optional equipment could be ordered for your Cub to tailor it to your needs. They included: adjustable-tread front axle, $21.75; belt pulley and PTO attachment, $37; swinging drawbar, $4.50; electric starting and lighting, $59.50; combination rear lamp and tail lamp, $4.50; spark arrestor, $6; muffler, $2.75; deluxe foam rubber upholstered seat, $8.25; touch control Hydraulic system, $84; front wheel weights, $6 per pair; and rear wheel weights $30.25 per pair. A similarly equipped Cub with electric starting and lighting, Touch Control Hydraulics, wheel weights

This view of a Cub with a mid-mounted cultivator clearly shows the lift linkage from the hydraulic lift-all unit. The cast-iron front wheel weights aided tractor steering. Fingertip control of the cultivator was accomplished with the lift-all control lever that the operator is touching. *State Historical Society of Wisconsin*

(one set front and rear), muffler, upholstered seat, adjustable front axle, and belt pulley/PTO was $867.

That was a lot of money in 1950, but it pales in comparison to the prices that Cub tractors can bring today in the marketplace. Today in the collector market completely restored Farmall Cubs can easily exceed triple the original price.

To accompany your new Cub, you needed Cub-specific implements. Using specifically designed implements meant that more work could be done in less time than using a larger oversized implement. IH offered a vast array of implements to fit your specific crop needs. A short list of these implements and their 1950 list prices include: #3 spring tooth field

cultivator, $61; 4-foot-wide #23A tandem disc harrow $134; Cub 33 two-row bean harvester, $55.50; Cub 22 4-foot-wide sickle mower $97; Cub 151 one-furrow disk plow $128; Cub 189 one-furrow 12-inch two-way moldboard plow $118; Cub leveling and grader blade $35; Cub two wheeled farm trailer with tires $174; and rear-mounted Cub tool bar $28.25 (ground

After the winter chill, the Cub could be used with a mid-mounted grading blade to level out the farmyard. Note the clear view of the blade the operator has, and the massive trip spring that protects the tractor from blade overload. This Cub also has a rare, electric hour meter attachment which is the round dial beside the control pedals. *State Historical Society of Wisconsin*

Serial Numbers for Farmall Cub Tractor Prefix Letters FCUB	
501 to 11347	Built in 1947
11348 to 57830	Built in 1948
57831 to 99535	Built in 1949
99536 to 121453	Built in 1950
121454 to 144454	Built in 1951
144455 to 162283	Built in 1952
162284 to 179411	Built in 1953
179412 to 186440	Built in 1954
186441 to 193657	Built in 1955
193658 to 198230	Built in 1956
198231 to 204388	Built in 1957
204389 to 211440	Built in 1958
211441 to 214973	Built in 1959
214974 to 217381	Built in 1960
217382 to 220037	Built in 1961
220038 to 221382	Built in 1962
221383 to 223452	Built in 1963
223453 to 224703	Built in 1964

A not-so-common use for the Cub was the rear-mounted buzz saw. Here two company men (real users would not wear suits or fedoras) pose for a photo. The use of this type of saw was once common, but safety regulations have since banished it to the scrap heap. *State Historical Society of Wisconsin*

tooling available at extra cost). These implements appear to be bargain-basement priced compared to their current replacements.

IH dealers often would deal in tractor and implement packages. For example, if you purchased the tractor and plow, the plow would be sold for less than list price or some other financial incentive to sweeten the deal and secure the sale. This time-honored method of dealing is still used today in many professions, but it is most typified in the sale of farm machinery.

A Variation Is Born: The International and Farmall Cub Lo-Boy

The Cub Lo-Boy was a variation of the Farmall Cub tractor. The Low Slung Farmall Cub was first shown at the Hinsdale, IL, Demonstration show held September 29-30, 1954. Farm Tractor Committee report Number 370, dated 12-21-1954 traces the development of the new Low Slung Farmall Cub that was referred to as the Cub Lo-Boy.

A stock Farmall Cub was the base unit used to build the prototype of the Low Slung tractor. Rotating the rear axle housings modified this Cub, thus lowering the tractor height by about 7 inches. The front axle extensions were also shortened accordingly to match. With the rear axle housing rotated forward, the tractor wheelbase was shortened to 62 1/2 inches as compared to the 69 1/4-inch wheelbase of the Farmall Cub.

The other modifications made to the prototype included moving the operator's seat to an area where it was nearly in line with the steering wheel. The seat would be made of sheet metal with foam rubber padding and a tilt-back feature. This was in contrast to the post-and-spring style seat on the Farmall Cub. This tip-over seat made operator entry/exit much easier. A step was also to be added to the tractor rear Fast Hitch arm and a new screw type

This close-up shot of a disk tiller attachment shows not only the disk and scraper, but also the hydraulic lift-all attachment. Note the tractor's hand starting crank under the drivers left shoe, the normal storage place for the crank. *State Historical Society of Wisconsin*

adjustment lever replaced the implement lever on the right side of the tractor. The Low Slung Cub could be mounted or dismounted from either the front or rear.

The transmission shift lever was also shortened and bent forward slightly for better operator control.

Due to the acceptance of the prototype by those who viewed it at the Hinsdale show, four more units were modified accordingly by the engineering department and sent to regional farm shows to gather more market interest data. Would the new Low Slung Cub hinder the Farmall Cub sales? How much new market share could IH gain by introducing this model? Were there any competitive designs that this could be directly marketed against? Would sale of the standard Cub be reduced? These were questions that IH needed to answer before mass production would begin.

Of the five prototypes built, the Farm Tractor Engineering Department kept two and three were sent to the Implement Works in Canton, Illinois. It was imperative that the Implement Works have implements ready to be used with this tractor when it was introduced for sale to the public.

With the Low Slung Cub, accessibility to drainage ditches for mowing would be vastly improved over the Farmall Cub, due to the lower center

The addition of the new, low-slung Cub, commonly called the Lo-Boy, added many new tractor sales to IH dealers. Here, a 1959-1963 styled Cub Lo-Boy is outfitted with turf tread tires and a sickle bar mower. With leaves on the ground, winter can't be too far away. *State Historical Society of Wisconsin*

of gravity. IH determined that most of the Cub Lo-Boys that would be made be sold primarily for mowing jobs. It was imperative that the allied equipment manufacturers have a lawn mowing attachment ready for the tractor introduction.

The uses for the new Lo-Boy were nearly as endless as those that the Farmall Cub could perform. Also, IH marketing thought that because the Cub Lo-Boy was to be used primarily by industrial or municipal entities, an electric horn was made as an available attachment. The Cub Lo-Boy was only offered with an under-slung exhaust system that exited the tractor near the left rear wheel. A vertical exhaust defeated the purpose of building a lowered tractor. The basic components of the tractor; engine, transmission, differential, and cowling were common to both the regular Cub and the Cub Lo-Boy.

The General sales department forecasted that if the Cub Lo-Boy were produced, over 2,500 units could easily be sold in 1955. This was in addition to the already projected sale of more than 10,000 Farmall Cub trac-

Winter arrived and the Lo-Boy found its niche in snowplowing duties. The front-mounted IH grading blade made quick work of even the biggest drifts. The Lo-Boy's three-speed transmission put the power to ground on even the slipperiest surfaces. Notice that this tractor does not have rear tire chains or weights. *State Historical Society of Wisconsin*

tors for 1955. The report states lastly that the name of this new tractor should be International Cub Lo-Boy. The International name was a new indicator of standard tread tractors like the International 600 and 650. These big brothers to the Cub Lo-Boy offered a fixed or very limited adjustment of the wheel tread or the tractor. The list price of the Cub

Lo-Boy in 1955 was $980, a fraction of the amount that these tractors command today in the marketplace.

The addition of the rear Fast Hitch allowed the 1955 and later built Cub and Cub Lo-Boy to be used with Fast Hitch implements such as the mold-board plow, disc harrow, and rear platform carrier attachments. The Cub Fast Hitch differed from the larger IH

tractor's Fast Hitch in that it only had a single hitch tongue receptacle centrally located at the rear of the tractor. Cub Lo-Boys and Cub tractors equipped with a Fast Hitch were known as 1-point-hitch tractors. The larger Farmall tractors had 2-hitch tongue receptacles. These tractors equipped with a Fast Hitch were known as two-point hitch tractors.

After the snow is gone and spring has passed, it's time to cultivate and weed. Cultivating offers many benefits to the soil—it reduces runoff by increasing the water absorption of the soil, and weeds can be removed without the use of chemicals. *State Historical Society of Wisconsin*

The implements that fit into these sockets have a specific thickness of hitching point or tongue. The 1-point tongue was shorter in height than the 2-point version. This measurable difference in size, kept operators from using non-Cub Fast Hitch adaptable implements on their tractors and thus prevented (hopefully) tractor overloading by the implement.

With a Fast Hitch the operator could back up to the implement, click the implement hitch tongue into the tractor hitch socket, and go. The operator never left the seat. Changing implements was never faster, or easier! The only drawback to the Fast Hitch system was the lack of hitch draft control. IH's main competitor (in implement hitching systems) was the

Ferguson system. This was found on the wildly popular Ford 2N, 8N and 9N tractors. It offered a crude draft control system that would automatically adjust the hitch to a preset level made by the operator. If IH engineers could devise a draft control system into the Fast Hitch, it would become the industries standard of implement to tractor attachment. However, IH refused to

When equipped with an optional rear Fast Hitch, IH's rear implement hitching system, the Cub becomes even more versatile. Here a single-gang Fast-Hitch disc harrow tills a path not much wider than the tractor. Today, Cub tractors equipped with the Fast Hitch are very collectible. *State Historical Society of Wisconsin*

release the Fast Hitch patents to the rest of industry and when the Ferguson patents expired, most tractor manufactures adopted this system. Allis-Chalmers also suffered a similar fate with their snap coupler rear hitching system in the 1960s.

Initially IH offered both a Farmall- and an International-style Lo-Boy. The basic difference was that the Farmall had an adjustable wide front tread axle, the International did not. IH dropped the adjustable front axle on the Lo-Boy in 1958, sales demand did not justify offering this item.

IH kept the Lo-Boy serial numbers recorded separately from the original Farmall Cub serial number list. When the Cub Lo-Boy was introduced, IH started production with serial number 501. When IH changed the body style of the Cub and Cub Lo-Boy, the serial numbers did not revert to 501. The Cub Lo-Boy service parts book notes the serial number breaks for the respective tractor body styles.

The Cub Lo-Boy was never offered with a wire mesh-style front grille that the original Farmall Cub, built from 1947 to 1954, featured. The 00- and

This garden is being quickly cultivated thanks to the Farmall Cub with its mid-mounted cultivator. This body type of the Cub was built from 1959 to 1963. Note the ample ground clearance the Cub affords; plant damage is greatly reduced because of this. *State Historical Society of Wisconsin*

50-series styled bar grilles were the only styles offered on the Cub Lo-Boy built in the 1950s. All of the first two generations of Cub Lo-Boy's were equipped with stainless steel emblems on their hoods. With the addition of white grille and white decals on the side of the hood as the major difference between the first and second generation of Cub Lo-Boys. The third and final generation of the Cub Lo-Boy used stamped-metal oval shaped plates for model identification and had a large horizontal three-bar front grille. These were similar in appearance to the 460-560 styled tractors of the same era. IH gave all of its Cubs and Cub Lo-Boys they built through 1963 styling similar to larger Farmall tractors that were being produced at the same time, giving a family appearance look. The Cub was first released in 1947 with a wire mesh grille and smooth sided hood with three horizontal bars stamped into the hood side for rigidity. This body style was retained until the 1954 tractor production year. Then the Cub and newly introduced Cub Lo-Boy shared the same hood with a new horizontal nine-bar grille. This hood has a wedge shaped depression stamped into its side directly above the engine. The tractors were built from 1954 to 1958. IH made two variations of these styled tractors.

This yellow-painted Cub Lo-Boy is being used for industrial work. Here a rear PTO-driven power trencher is working hard to dig a trench where utility cables will be buried. The small size of the Cub Lo-Boy made it ideal for tight jobs such as this. *State Historical Society of Wisconsin*

All Cubs made from serial number 185,000 to 210,000 and Cub Lo-Boys from serial number 501 to 10,000 have stainless steel emblems attached to the side of the hood identifies the tractor model . After 1956, the indentation on the side of the tractor hood had an added white decal that was a background for the letters. This was to emulate the red and white paint scheme IH was using on its agricultural tractors, the 350 and 450. Much confusion has surrounded the 1954-1959 styled stainless Cub tractor family. The largest mistake is the thought that these tractors had model identification decals. This is not true. The only decals on the stainless tractors are the white hood background, used on the 1957 to 1959 built tractors, and the various caution/warning decals found on all of the machines. At one time, IH offered the stainless emblems in decal form through their service parts division, but they have since been retired.

One important distinguishing feature that all of the Cub and Cub Lo-Boy tractors with the stainless emblems have is in their electrical system. IH used a two-wire sealed beam headlight in these machines. To distinguish the sealed beam lights from the older style, note both the wiring and the shape of the light housing. The sealed beam lights have two wires leading to them and their metal housings have a flat profile or "pie pan." The older-style lights are often referred to as the bullet-style lights due to their unique bullet shaped housing. Both styles of lights were a product of the Guide Light Company that is now owned by the AC-Delco division of General Motors. All of the headlights and taillights offered by IH were always painted to match the tractor; they did not paint them black.

Double duty on the graveyard shift is the appropriate title for these two Cub Lo-Boys with center-mounted rotary mowers. The clear view of the work area and the nimble handling of the Lo-Boy made these tractors a favorite for these types of jobs. *State Historical Society of Wisconsin*

This overhead view shows several highway-orange Cub Lo-Boys with side-mounted sickle bar mowers. This appears to be a highway department storage yard with several other industrial IH tractors parked near by. Orange-painted tractors were an extra charge, factory option that IH offered. *State Historical Society of Wisconsin*

Another note about the electrical system is that all Cubs prior to serial number 224401 and Cub Lo-Boys prior to serial number 18701 were made with a 6-volt positive ground electrical system. (By mid 1964, IH modernized it to a 12-volt negative ground system.)

The two holes in the hood of the Cub on the right side are access holes to the generator bearings. Because the generator is tucked under the hood, and the hood does not have a flip open access door, IH engineers added the two holes to allow the operator to add two or three drops of 20W oil using a oil can to the bearing caps of the generator. To find a Cub or Cub Lo-Boy with the stainless emblems intact today can be quite rare and reproduction emblems expensive. The average list price for a 1950s vintage Cub Lo-Boy was $1,100. Today a Cub Lo-Boy in good mechanical and physical condition can bring three or four times that original amount.

Serial Numbers for Farmall and International Cub Lo-Boy Tractor	
501 to 2554	Built in 1955
2555 to 3928	Built in 1956
3929 to 6581	Built in 1957
6582 to 10566	Built in 1958
10567 to 12370	Built in 1959
12371 to 13903	Built in 1960
13904 to 15505	Built in 1961
15506 to 16439	Built in 1962
16440 to 17927	Built in 1963
17928 to 19405	Built in 1964
19406 to 21175	Built in 1965
21176 to 23114	Built in 1966
23115 to 24480	Built in 1967
24481 to 26007	Built in 1968

CHAPTER 3

HIGHER HORSEPOWER AND NEW COLORS OF THE INTERNATIONAL LO-BOYS

In the 1960s, International Harvester (IH) made more changes to the Cub and Cub Lo-Boy lines than any other time in their history. Not only were new body styles created, but a new design of the Lo-Boy line was engineered that was radically different from the original versions. And the Farmall version of the Cub was retired.

On March 31, 1960 IH replaced the familiar red paint it had been using on the Cub Lo-Boy with 483 federal Yellow. IH thought that yellow was a standard accepted color, was more visible at night, and appeared to buyers to make the machine look larger, thus creatingindustrial sales. Also, every other large industrial machinery manufacture offered yellow painted equipment and IH didn't want to be left out. The Farmall Cub version offered 483 yellow as an optional color choice, with IH red the standard color.

With a mighty 60-inch-wide mowing deck underneath, a Cub 154 Lo-Boy powers up a steep hill with ease. The 154 Lo-Boys low center of gravity made it an ideal mowing tractor on slopes and in less than ideal terrain.

The offset seat of the Cub offered Cultivision, as IH termed it. This view of a 1959-1963-production Cub shows that feature a straight-ahead unblocked view of the work you were doing. This field looks to be too damp to cultivate, but the Cub is doing a fine job. *State Historical Society of Wisconsin*

The Cub and Cub Lo-Boy were restyled in 1959 to copy the IH 460-560 tractors that also were released. These tractors had a larger 3 horizontal bar grille that was painted IH white along with the tractor's model designation in a stamped metal oval located on the side supports of the front grille housing. The tractors were still bathed in IH red, but were now accented in IH white. The Cubs from serial number 210,001 (1958) to 222,500 (1963) were styled like this, as were the Cub Lo-Boy's from serial number 1001 to 17200.

The Farmall Cubs received their last styling face lift in 1964 with a new flat grille housing and new paint. The grille gave the tractor a squared look at the front end. The grille screen, hood, wheel rims, and grille housing were now IH white with the balance of the tractor painted IH 483 Federal Yellow. This flat grille style would be retained by IH (with some minor color and decal changes) until it was retired in 1979. The last Cub Lo-Boy with the square grille was serial number 26007 built in 1968. The model 154 Cub Lo-Boy replaced this that same year.

IH effectively killed the Farmall Cub with the release of Tractor Committee

Serial Number Listings for International Cub Tractor	
224704 to 225109	Built in 1964
225110 to 227208	Built in 1965
227209 to 229224	Built in 1966
229225 to 231004	Built in 1967
231005 to 232980	Built in 1968
232981 to 234867	Built in 1969
234868 to 236826	Built in 1970
236827 to 238505	Built in 1971
238506 to 240580	Built in 1972
240581 to 242745	Built in 1973
242746 to 245650	Built in 1974
245651 to 248124	Built in 1975

The Farmall Cub and Cub Lo-Boy were the only IH tractors to have a a unique rear-implement hitch. The Fast Hitch differed from the agricultural tractor in that one hitch tongue was used, not two. Here, an operator gets ready to click-and-go with a Fast Hitch moldboard plow. Oddly, the plow coulter still needs to be attached. *State Historical Society of Wisconsin*

Report #141 dated 5-25-1964. It stated that when the Cub was originally introduced, it was primarily used on small farms, but with the trend of farm consolidation and mergers, the demand for Cubs steadily declined. Industrial use of Cubs increased steadily and accounted for 75 percent of the annual sales of the Cub tractor.

Because the majority of the Cub sales were to industrial users, the International version of the Cub was retained and the Farmall agricultural version was retired for the first time. IH offered the International version of the Cub only in its Federal Yellow and IH white paint scheme. This color change would not hinder any sales to agricultural customers, or would overseas sales be affected. This change took place in 1963.

The International Cub was built starting in 1964 with serial number 224704 to serial number 248124, which ended in 1975. The initial list price of the International Cub in 1964 was $1,680; in 1975, when it was dropped from the IH tractor line, that list price had doubled to $3,529. It is interesting to note that while a vertical exhaust system was available on the International Cub, the IH sales literature of the time never showed this feature.

The company's products were manufactured in one country for distribution in several others. The Cubs and Cub Lo-Boys sold in the North American market had decal insignia on them stating McCormick Farmall Cub or International Cub. An export tractor might have McCormick International Farmall Cub on its hood

because those sold in offshore markets still had registered trade names in their respective countries of sale that were used. It's amazing to think that with all of the trademark names that IH had registered around the world that a label with all of these trade names even fit on the side of the Cub's short hood.

International Numbered Lo-Boys

IH made three major versions of the Lo-Boy. The first generation of the Cub Lo-Boy was a Farmall Cub that had been reduced in both overall height and wheelbase. These shared the same external styling as the Farmall Cubs.

The second major model versions were the Cub 154 Lo-Boy and Cub 185 Lo-Boy. These tractors retained the IH-built 4-cylinder L head designed liquid cooled engine and the transmission/final drive unit of the original Cub Lo-Boy. Changes included the addition of improved hydraulics, automotive style steering, formed channel steel frame, completely new grille and hood styling, and the operator's seat was relocated to a position in line with the driveline from the engine.

A deluxe seat, plenty of leg-room, and a clear view of the work ahead were all features of this 1959-1963-styled Cub. The rear-mounted Fast Hitch plow was hydraulically raised and lowered by a fingertip control lever. *State Historical Society of Wisconsin*

The cast-metal clutch housing (which contained the drive clutch and transmission shaft) was eliminated. The new numbered Lo-Boys started with a starter/generator, similar in style to those later found on the IH Cub Cadet. The Starter/generator would act as the cranking motor for the engine and then convert into the tractor generator during tractor operation. The numbered Lo-Boys were increased in engine horsepower from 9 horsepower on the original Cub Lo-Boy to 15 horsepower on the 154 and eventually peaked at 18 horsepower on the 185 and 184 Cub Lo-Boy models.

The third version was the 184 Cub Lo-Boy. This has been considered the most refined of the Lo-Boy series, because it used an actual bendix-driven starter motor to engage the engine. Batteries were charged with an engine driven alternator. It was painted IH 2150 red and 935 white and had the basic styling appearance of the IH 86 series farm tractors.

The Model 154 Cub Lo-Boy

The release of the 154 in 1968 was a major change for the IH Cub Lo-Boy line. A totally new design of tractor framework was used. This style of frame would be retained by IH until the Lo-Boy was retired in 1979. The IH Farm Equipment Committee Report #249 dated 1-11-68, and approved on 2-23-68, released the new International Cub 154 Lo Boy tractor and its companion 60-inch rotary mower for regular production. The reports states that "Trends of buyers and applications indicate a potential for lawn and garden tractors larger than our present 12 horsepower Cadet. This potential exists for a tractor with modern styling and more convenience features at a lower price than our International Cub tractor."

"The present Cub tractor was introduced approximately 20 years ago primarily for agricultural purposes. With changing practices, the demand for a Cub tractor as a farm tractor has declined and the demand for the Industrial Cub has increased. There are certain design characteristics of the Cub that necessitate compromises when used for Industrial applications-namely operators convenience and comfort, visibility, mounting of companion equipment and others."

IH built two prototypes of the 154 Cub Lo Boy and sent one to Belleglade, FL, for experimental field-testing. The other was used for both laboratory and production tooling tests. Laboratory testing was conducted with satisfactory results on both the new engine, and PTO clutches. Production was slated to begin in October 1968.

This new tractor was equipped with a modified IH-built C-60 engine, and a modified final drive unit. The engine was basically the same used in the present Cub tractor, modified to achieve a 15 horsepower output at 2,200 rpm by using improved crankshaft bearings, aluminum pistons, improved valves with rotators

Outfitted with a Danco-brand front-mounted snow blower, this Cub cleans up the driveway in a short time. The torque of the C-60 engine in the Cub helps cut big drifts down to size. This snow blower is driven by a shaft to the rear PTO of the tractor. *State Historical Society of Wisconsin*

included on the exhaust valves, and a new manifold. The engine cooling system remained the same. A thermosyphon radiator with an area of 1.4 square feet along with a 2-row core would allow full engine cooling in 114-degree air. A horizontally mounted muffler with side exhaust outlet was standard equipment. A vertical exhaust was not offered. The higher rpm of the engine help it to develop more horsepower than the previous International Cub Lo-Boy.

The 154 were the first Cub Lo-Boy to use a replaceable dry type cartridge air filter element. IH used two different types of air filter elements on the 154. The 185 and 184 used an element common to the earlier 154 style.

Because of the higher engine rpm (2,200 versus 1,800), higher ground

speeds could be expected that would improve mowing operation speeds.

The Cub 154 Lo-Boy differed from it predecessor the Cub Lo-Boy because it used a Delco-Remy combination starter/generator instead of a bendix-driven starter. This connected to the engine via a single V belt drive between the crankshaft, cooling fan, and starter-generator. The electrical system was rated 12-volt. The 12-volt battery was located behind the operator near the right rear fender. Twin sealed beam headlamps were recessed above the tractor grille and an optional rear combination red and white rear lamp was available. Ignition was accomplished by key-type starting with a safety-starting switch on the clutch pedal. The C-60 engine was equipped with an IH-built distributor with an automatic spark advance.

Because the operator now straddled the transmission (similar to the Cub Cadet) a new steering mechanism needed to be developed. IH used an Ackerman-type steering gearbox with a 13:1 ratio. A 15-inch steering wheel with a center point of control of the front axle tie rods achieved a 9.4-foot turning radius without braking. A cast iron, center pivoted, front axle absorbed shock loads and added rigidity to the tractor.

The drive train of the 154 was the same as the current model Cub Lo-Boy. However, the PTO drive was through a pulley on the engine clutch shaft; a set of matched belts drove the PTO shaft. This shaft extended under the transmission to a rear clutch to provide a rear PTO. The use of a multiple disc dry-type clutch provided a rear PTO speed of 1,830 rpm at 2,200 engine rpm. The PTO was independent, meaning that it would continue to operate even if the main clutch pedal was depressed. If a tough mowing spot were encountered the operator could stop the tractor without interrupting engine power to the mower. This is particularly helpful when using a snow blower and short movements of the tractor is needed.

IH's Louisville Works encountered a manufacturing quagmire that caused about 25 percent of the 154's to suffer driveline failure. The assembly tolerances set forth by the engineering department were too stringent and caused clutch shaft failures. When the handmade prototypes were built, this defect was not discovered because production-tooling jigs were not being used. IH made changes to the assembly process and tooling, and corrected the defective tractors in inventory and in the field.

The tractor frame was a major change from previous models because it was comprised of two full-length sheet steel formed channel members. This framed Lo-Boy did not use the heavy cast torque tube as the previous Lo-Boys had. By using a straight channel frame, the mounting of allied equipment such as front-end loaders, blades, and brooms would be greatly simplified. The steel disc rear wheels had a fixed tread design, unlike that used on the previous Cub Lo-Boys. The engine power was still delivered to the transmission by a driveshaft.

The transmission and final drive were the same as those used on previous International Cub Lo-Boys. The 154 came with 4.00-12 ribbed front tires and 8.3-24 rear agricultural bar-tread style tires. Optional 20x8-10 terra front tires and 13.6-16 turf style rear tires for the tractors commonly set up for yard, or lawn work.

The 154 used the same operator seat as the Cub Cadet 122, 123, 124, and 125. The seat was solid mounted with the provision for fore and aft positioning by using selective holes in the seat support. The new seat support attached to the rear fenders instead of the rear axle housing, as was the case in previous models, for added rigidity.

One of the major improvements the 154 had over its predecessor was the addition of an instrument panel dash. As IH author Guy Fay says "it's a tractor with *DASH*!!" This is where the engine throttle and choke control levers were located. Both of these were now automotive-style push-pull cables like those used on the Cub Cadet. The key starting switch and optional horn button were also located here. An oil Tellite was also located on the dash to alert the operator of any situations in which low engine oil pressure may be

detected. Separate levers to control the rear hitch, hydraulic lift and independent PTO also were conveniently located within the operator's reach. Because of the restyling changes, the 154 looked like a modern tractor; because it was.

This wasn't just an old tractor with a new skin; IH had made some major design changes to the 154 to make it a new tractor. It is ironic that the 154 was considered an industrial tractor, yet it did not resemble any of IH industrial tractors of the time. The tractor it most resembled was the IH 4100 4-wd tractor.

A major change with the 154 was its new hydraulic system. An engine-mounted 2 gallons-per-minute pump rated at 2,000 psi supplied oil to a fixed one-way cylinder to operate the front lifting rockshaft. A full-flow, replaceable, spin-on-type hydraulic oil filter was easy to service unlike the mesh screen in previous models. A rear-mounted 3-point hitch with position control provided a lift capacity of 450 pounds. A nudging-type control valve operated this hitch. This new system, often referred to as Touch Control, replaced the old cast iron cylinder block found on the previous Lo-Boy models. A hand operated lift that provided similar lifting effort to the smaller Cub Cadets was optional.

The 154 offered a choice of either a rigid rear drawbar, or a 3-point hitch for tractors that were equipped with hydraulic lift.

Oddly, the 154 Cub Lo-Boy was offered in three different body styles but the only difference were the product graphic (decal) packages.

The first style of 154 was used prior to serial number 14535. This tractor had a white hood with a light blue decal on the length of the hood. The model number 154 was at the rear of the stripe near the instrument cowling. These tractors also had a yellow grille surround and white padded vinyl seat with blue piping trim and the mesh grille screen was painted silver. These were built approximately 1968 to early 1969.

The second or intermediate style was used on serial number 14536 to serial number 18708. This was approximately 1969 and 1970.

The third style was used on serial number 18709 and out. These styled Cubs were built from 1970 until the 154 was replaced with the model 185 in 1974. The 154 used a black decal stripe with a blue pinstripe border. A vinyl-padded black seat and vertically ribbed front grille screen were characteristic of this model variation.

On all of the 154 Lo-Boy tractors, the basic styling of the hood and grille remained . Only the accentual striping was changed to match the Cub Cadet striping scheme to give the 154 the IH family appearance.

IH had planned to test and market (at a later date) a hydrostatic drive transmission in the 154. A complete hydrostatic transmission of the size and cost needed for the 154 was currently not available in the industry. Hydro vendors would however, approve the use of current units when combined with the usage of supplemental gearing. The 154 hydro would be a component tractor. The tractor manufacturer (IH) would use parts or components from outside vendors in combination with its own manufactured parts to build the final product. The exact specifications of this tractor elude this author. However one could venture to guess that if IH engineers wanted to take this tractor "one step further" they easily could have.

The best way to sell tractors is to demonstrate! This is exactly what this IH dealer is doing. A red Farmall Cub and a yellow International Cub Lo-Boy show their abilities in handling the Danco front-mounted snow blower. *State Historical Society of Wisconsin*

This author is alluding to a Cub Lo-Boy with a hydro-mechanical transmission. Here the three-speed transmission would be coupled to a hydrostatic drive unit. This would produce infinitely variable speeds in three ranges. The reverse gear would be removed from the mechanical transmission, as the hydro would control the machine direction. For some reason—most likely the cost of production—IH never pursued the Lo Boy Hydro tractor version.

Another odd version that IH planned but never made was the 154 High Clearance tractor. While the specifications of this machine are yet to be found, this author would venture to estimate that the 154 Hi Clearance could have replaced the International Cub. The 154's hood and grille styling would have been retained however, the rail frame of the 154 may have been replaced by the cast torque tube that the Cub used to connect the engine to the transmission. IH studied this tractor in 1967, but it was never built, nor is there evidence that IH actually built a 154 Hi Clearance prototype tractor.

IH built 29,171 copies of the 154 Cub Lo-Boy during its production run from 1968 to 1974. None of the numbered series of Cub Lo-Boys (154, 184, and 185) were ever tested at the

IH held several field days every year to demonstrate new products. Here, a small sampling of the IH industrial line is being presented. Shown are several 2404 industrial tractors, a T-340 crawler loader, and in the foreground, a Cub Cadet Original and an International Cub Lo-Boy tractor, both with mounted rotary mowers. Note the extra spare tractor parts near the tent. *State Historical Society of Wisconsin*

Nebraska Tractor Testing facility in Lincoln, NE. The original list price for a 154 Cub Lo-Boy was $1,788 in 1968. These were sold exclusively through the 3,600 IH dealers located nationwide in the United States and in several foreign branches.

IH offered a wide range of approved implements designed specifically for the 154, including:

- 54-inch Front Mounted Blade
- Model 3142 under mounted 42 inch cutting width Rotary Cutter
- Model 48 under mounted 48 inch cutting width Rotary Mower
- 60 inch Cut Under Mounted Rotary Mower
- Model 3160 Under Mounted 60 inch cutting width Rotary Cutter
- Model 3260 Under Mounted 60 inch cutting width Rotary Mower
- 110 Tandem Disc Harrow
- 1050A Hydraulic Front End Loader
- 222 Sickle Bar Mower
- 310 Moldboard Plow
- Model 15 Rear Mounted Rotary Tiller
- Model 50 Front Mounted Snow Blower

All weather cab in either full metal or combination metal with vinyl curtains.

All of these implements were painted in IH white and labeled as an International product and came with a warranty. Rotary cutter and rotary mowers are not the same. Rotary cutters offer a higher cutting height adjustment and are made for rough cut areas such as road ditches. Rotary mowers or finish mowers are built for fine manicuring a lawn. Rotary mowers appear to be more lawnmower style in appearance. Also, rotary mowers were offered as an attachment, adjustable height gauge wheels, whereas the rotary cutter had only adjustable height skid shoes.

Many allied equipment manufactures built implements to fit the 154 Cub Lo-Boy. One of the more notable aftermarket companies that still exist today is the Woods Company of Oregon, IL. Woods built mowing decks for the 154 and hundreds of other tractor model applications. It is often confusing to many 154 owners as to who built their mower deck. The IH 3142 mower deck is a near knock off of the Woods model 42 mower. Both have a unique octagon mower deck housing shape, but their parts are not interchangeable. They are often confused with each other due to their similar housing shape.

For all of the brawn the 154 gave in appearance, the model 50 snow thrower was still only a single stage machine. Its huge, 24-inch-diameter auger could eat the largest of glaciers fast, and with its optional side extension plates the cutting width was

Serial Number Listings for International Cub 154 Lo-Boy Tractors	
7505 to 8272	Built in 1968
8273 to 15501	Built in 1969
15502 to 20331	Built in 1970
20332 to 23342	Built in 1971
23343 to 27537	Built in 1972
27538 to 31765	Built in 1973
31766 to 36676	Built in 1974

increased from 54 to 60 inches. A reversible cutting edge and adjustable skid shoes that its little brother, the Cub Cadet, used on its snow throwers were standard equipment. The snow thrower was lifted through the tractors hydraulic lift to a height of up to 6 inches. This snow thrower could throw snow up to 25 feet away.

IH's competitors were offering garden tractors in the 14 horsepower range when compared to the Cub Lo-Boy 154. John Deere was selling the model 140, which was a 14 horsepower garden tractor that had been upgraded from a 12 horsepower model in 1969. Bolens offered its model 1455, which was basically a 14 horsepower upgrade from their 12 horsepower model 1250. J. I. Case sold its model 444 hydraulic drive tractor, which offered no basic design changes from their 12 horsepower model 442. The Wheel Horse Company's model GT 14 was smaller than the 154 and offered a 48-inch mower deck. None of the other OEM's had a model that compared to the 154. IH once again had found its tractor niche market.

CHAPTER 4

CUB CADET CONCEPT, DEVELOPMENT, AND HISTORY

The story of the Cub Cadet line actually starts several years before the tractor hit the yards of North America. In 1959, International Harvester (IH) recognized that the urban customer market for a durable, multi-purpose garden tractor had arrived. A few companies had already entered this fledgling market, but IH saw the great untapped market potential that could attract both urban and commercial customers into its vast nationwide network of dealers. The farmer (IH's main customer) could find many uses for a small tractor including grass mowing and snow removal around the farmstead. Commercial landscape and grounds keepers (golf courses, estates, and government park districts) also

A Cub Cadet Original is shown moving the batting cage at Chicago's Wrigley Field, home of the appropriately named Cubs. IH used the Cub Cadet in many high-profile venues to attract public attention, and thereby, generate sales. You could say that IH hit a Grand Slam with the Cub Cadet tractor.

Here is where it all starts, on the tractor assembly line. This IH employee of the Louisville Works is installing the steering column assembly prior to the tractor being painted. Note the special alignment fixtures used to accomplish this. *State Historical Society of Wisconsin*

would be huge potential buyers of this machine. IH enjoyed having a reputation for durable, well-engineered products, along with an expansive dealer network and parts warehousing system to support it. Sales and service for your Cub Cadet could be found at the local IH dealer in town, not three counties away as with some of the other manufactures in the market.

Now that IH knew the market it wanted to enter, it needed a product to do this with. Should they buy a product already out on the market through an acquisition or build their own? IH executives attending a farm show in 1957 saw the Bolens garden tractor and quickly realized that IH could sell many of these types of tractors. Accessing its tractor lineup, IH management decided that components of the Farmall Cub tractor could be used to build a scaled down machine. The Cub was essentially a two-thirds scale Farmall A, so why not scale down the Cub too? IH decided to use selected components of the Cub tractor including the transmission/differential housing and the Cub hood/gas tank as basic parts. This parts commonality would keep the net cost of production low for IH, allow the Cub tooling to be used for a second purpose, and also facilitate a reduced product development/ startup time. A newly designed steel channel frame and cast iron front axle, along with a Kohler Engine Company gasoline powered engine would be added to form the basic machine. After a prototype was built, it was decided to abandon the Cub hood/ fuel tank because it made the unit too long and bulky, and replace it with a new IH design.

On July 29, 1960 IH officially approved the project of building a 7 horsepower urban use tractor that was subsequently called the International Cub Cadet. Some of the other names that IH had thought of using were Ranch All, Cub-Ette or Cub Urban. All three names were representative of the end user of the new tractor. The urban and ranch customer would be the primary consumer of this product.

This machine would prove to be a milestone for IH both in engineering and marketing. By using the basic Cub tractor transmission and differential, a large cost savings could be immediately achieved by not having to design a totally new drive train. Purchasing a small gasoline powered engine from an outside vendor (Kohler) made sense too. IH didn't have the time or engineering staff to develop a small power plant and still build a cost-effective tractor.

The IH Tractor Engineering Department was in charge of the Cub Cadet tractor development. They hand-built three Cub Cadet prototypes at the newly completed Engineering Center in Hinsdale, IL, (Now a suburb of Chicago, it was then a farming town) for testing from the initial design specifications developed in August of 1960. IH decided to build the Cub Cadet at the Louisville, KY, Works which was also where the Cub and Cub Lo-Boy tractors were made. Another assembly line was made, and the main drive train parts could be easily shuttled from the Cub production lines to the Cub Cadet line. A foundry was located on site that made the basic castings for both the Cub tractors, and the Cub Cadet drive train and front axle.

The Louisville Works was instructed by IH to build 10 prototype production models between October 5 and 14, 1960 to test manufacturing and assembly methods. Of these 10 first shot Cub Cadets built, six were placed with prospective customers in Hinsdale, IL, and adjacent neighborhoods in late October, to obtain maximum operation in the hands of users. IH wanted questionnaires to be filled out by each user giving their opinions and comments about their acceptability of the Cub Cadet tractor operating various implements, such as the rotary mower, blade, dump cart, etc., which were also made available to these users.

IH distributed the remaining four of the 10 prototypes as follows; one each to Consumer Relations, and the Farm Equipment Service Section, for photos and advertising materials, and service manual data respectively, and two were assigned to the Special Duty Development Committee. The Special Duty Development Committee was in charge of the designing and developing of the attachments to be used with the Cub Cadet tractors. All four were to be returned to IH Engineering at Hinsdale for the tentative introduction of the Cub Cadet line on November 19 to IH Company personnel. Oddly, it appears that the first 10 Cub Cadets built either had no production serial numbers assigned to them or were QC/QFE Hinsdale tagged units.

IH approved several special duty attachments for use with the Cub Cadet line from outside suppliers. These included the moldboard plow, disk harrow, and cultivator manufactured by Brinly-Hardy Company, a pull-type reel mower from Sunflower Industries, a trailing lawn sweeper made by Lambert Inc., a trailing seeder/fertilizer spreader from Schneider Metal Manufacturing, a pull-type lawn rake from Robbie Rake Company, and a trailing lawn roller and lawn aerator from Kenisco Manufacturing.

In November 1960 IH decided to test the waters again by building another limited production lot of 25 Cub Cadets at the Louisville Works. These were all to be equipped with an electric starter and an engine hour recording device. They were placed into the hands of users for field-testing and to determine the district, dealer and customer acceptance prior to the release for further full-scale production. IH needed more real world experience on

the Cub Cadets, this time with commercial users. (During the dead of winter in the Midwest, IH could not get the numbers of hours on the Cub Cadets that they needed for engineering research.) Thus, with a second batch of Cub Cadets, they could be equipped with the improvements already revised into the basic design and subjected to actual field conditions.

After contacting its Southern Regional Management, IH determined the ideal place to test Cub Cadets in the winter was in the southern states of the United States. IH engineering decided that of he 25 Cub Cadets used for testing, 25 were outfitted with mowers and 10 with front mounted blades that would be tested at the same time. These tractors, were given to users in areas where they received the most service in the shortest amount of time. A good example of potential users were be golf courses, sod farms, or government institutions.

From this lot of 25 tractors, IH engineering retained two tractors, two mowers, and one blade. The IH District Office at Phoenix, AZ received three tractors, three mowers and one blade. The balance of 20 tractors, 20 mowers and eight blades will be distributed by the IH southern sales region for field testing, near the Jacksonville, FL, Atlanta, GA, New Orleans, LA, and Birmingham, AL district territories.

IH needed a minimum of 50 hours mowing and or blade work on each unit. IH district reps tracked the progress of the units in their area and submitted weekly follow-up reports to IH engineering. At the conclusion of the testing period, the tractors were sold by the district offices for the best possible price. IH estimated the

The Transmission assembly line at Louisville Works assembled the Cub and Cub Cadet transmissions on the same line. The Cub transmissions had the straight shifting lever, the LoBoys had a bent lever; both had a long pilot shaft extending from the gear case. The Cub Cadet transmissions in the middle-background all have bent shifting levers but no rear PTO shaft. The Cub Cadet shared the same basic transmission with the larger Cub tractor. *State Historical Society of Wisconsin*

timetable to complete these tests to be around four to six weeks.

After this limited production lot of 25 tractors was produced for field testing in late November 1960, production of the Cub Cadet continued on a limited basis at the Louisville Works to test manufacturing equipment and procedures and to establish piecework prices. The actual retail shipments to

The 7 horsepower Kohler K-161 engine in the Original made it the ideal small industrial tractor for any business. An Original outfitted with a Danco snow thrower makes a quick winter cleanup at a suburban motel parking lot.

the various sales territories did not occur until after the successful run of field testing on these 25 units with their implements.

The Tractor Committee Report #49-A dated January 1, 1961 gave IH a quick update on the progress of the 25 Cub Cadets sent to the southern U.S. for field testing. The committee enthusiastically praised the performance of the Cub Cadet along with its companion rotary mower and front blade attachments. All of the 25 test units were placed with industrial type users to insure the maximum amount of operation and the greatest amount of diversification.

IH found through these tests that, "In the mowing of fairways and roughs, it was found that the cog-type belt used to drive the mower spindles was too loose, indicating the need for the provision of a tightening device. The tightener has since been provided and will be incorporated on the regular production units." A vital improvement to the mower deck that was necessary to the success of the Cub Cadet line was found before mass production (and sales) began. The report further states "Indications are that more of these machines will be sold for industrial use than was originally anticipated. In view of this, it is proposed to provide industrial attachments for both the rotary mower and the blade to protect the tractor and implements from damage such as would occur from high impact loads. In the case of the blade, this attachment would consist of an optional spring trip mechanism of a type similar to that

provided on tractor-mounted snow blades. The attachment as proposed for the rotary cutter would consist of a heavy-duty timing belt and the provision of swinging blades in lieu of the standard rigid type, thereby permitting the cutter to be used without damage to the machine in applications where rocks, pipes, and other foreign material are encountered."

The report also states the good performance and excellent acceptance of the Cub Cadets by the dealers and users, and recommends that (even though the 50 hour testing period is not completed yet) the release for shipment of production Cub Cadet units be issued at this time.

The serial numbers of the test units and their testing locations are:

501, 502	Miami, Florida
503	The Gator Bowl, Jacksonville, Florida
504, 514	Park District, Fort Pierce, Florida
505	Tifton, Georgia
506	Park Department, Orlando, Florida
507	Atlanta, Georgia
509	McCoy Air Force Base, Pinecastle, Florida
511, 515	Albany, Georgia
512	Cleveland Heights Country Club, Lakeland, Florida
517	Nilo Plantation, Albany, Georgia
518	Pineland Plantation, Albany, Georgia

Whether these units still reside at these locations is anyone's guess. Although, a few engineers may have taken the prototypes home to use in they're own yards, for real world testing on a personal level.

Whether you had a picture-perfect yard or just some weeds to cut, the 38-inch-wide mower deck for the Original helped cut any job down to size. Even women preferred the Original to other brands; its controls were operator friendly to everyone.

The topic of product identification (painting and decals) has always been an area of discussion. The IH Tractor Committee Report #49, dated September 29, 1960, states the Cub Cadet color dilemma best; "Recommendation is made to the Product Identification Committee that wheels, seat, grille screen and hood be painted Harvester White; the shifter knob, steering wheel, foot rests and control buttons are to be black; balance of tractor is to be painted Federal Yellow with Harvester Red as

optional." The report further states; "This recommendation is made by the fact that when customers were contacted during tests, many stated they would want tractors painted with the Harvester basic red and white combination whereas others indicated a preference for the yellow and white color combination. In addition, industrial dealers will prefer the yellow and white color combination and agricultural dealers will undoubtedly prefer the red and white combination . . . In meeting of October

13, tractors displaying both color combinations were viewed by the product committee and divisional product committee members and it was the consensus that both color combinations should be made available to satisfy this reaction of the customers. Louisville Works advises that they are prepared to provide both color combinations without additional cost."

A post note on Tractor Committee Report #49 states "The Divisional Product Committee is in agreement

Clearing a playground or lot was fast when you teamed a Cub Cadet Original with a Sweepster front-mounted broom. The dual rear wheels were an extra cost option that added stability to the tractor. It never was this easy to get a clean sweep without using a Cub Cadet!

with this report, with the exception of the recommendation of Harvester Red as an optional color. We request that this option be eliminated and tractors be introduced with color combination of yellow and white as approved by Product Identification Committee." Thus, until the 82 Series Cub Cadets were introduced in 1979, Cub Cadets were painted a familiar IH 483 or IH 483B Yellow and IH 901, IH 902, or IH 935 White. This is the trademark yellow/white color combination that still exists on Cub Cadets built today.

The Cub Cadet Original

The first model Cub Cadet actually did not have a model number associated with it. It was simply known as the International Cub Cadet Tractor or as it is more commonly known as, the Original. The reason this tractor became known as the Original was that it was the first or Original Cub Cadet tractor. The Original was powered by a single cylinder, 7 horsepower, model K-161 Kohler engine. This engine is easily recognized by the fact that it is the only Cub Cadet tractor to have an oil bath air cleaner on the engine. The tractor could be equipped with either recoil (rope pull) starting or electric starting. Electric starting was accomplished with the use of a combination starter/generator motor made for IH by the Delco-Remy Company. Several versions of the Delco starter generator were used in the next 10 years on Cub Cadets, but all of these motors are interchangeable with each other. The improvements made to the starter/generator include replacing the generator shaft bushings with ball bearings, heavier armature windings, improved brushes,

Many other machinery manufacturers offered implements that would fit on the Original. One such implement was a front-mounted mowing deck. This youngster seems to be making great progress on his mowing job with his Original that is outfitted with optional rear fenders.

increased torque production, and general reliability improvements.

All of the Originals have a pulley at the rear of the engine that allows a belt to connect the engine to the transmission clutch/driveshaft below it. Only the Original had a transmission driving system like this. All of the future Cub Cadets used a direct coupling at the engine for the transmission driveshaft. Depressing a pedal with the operators left foot operated the clutch. By depressing the pedal half way down, the drive clutch would release and the transmission would stop. When the pedal is fully depressed, the brake for the tractor is applied.

The transmission of the Original was a simple three-speed forward and single reverse speed. This was the same transmission used in its big brothers the Farmall Cub and Cub Lo-Boy. The shifting lever was angled

forward for operator comfort just as the Lo-Boy's was. The transmission produced forward speeds of 2.3, 3.1 and 6.9 miles per hour in first, second, and third gear, respectively. Reverse speed was 2.6 miles per hour. An optional creeper gear reduction gearbox was available that offered even slower speeds in all speeds. This was especially helpful when using a front mounted snow blower, or rear mounted tiller or moldboard plow where first gear was too fast. This gear reduction box was mounted ahead of the transmission and operated by a single cast iron lever directly ahead of the transmission shifter. The gearbox had two ranges, direct and under drive. The gearbox model UD9-6 was made by the Danco Company and was recommended to be used with the Danco-built snow blower model BB36.

The dog days of summer meant lounging by the pool. If you had a Cub Cadet Original in your yard, you could have more pool time. This reflective photo shows an Original outfitted with a 38-inch mower deck and optional dual rear wheels. The duallies offered extra stability and traction on slopes. This youngster appears to be thinking about the extra pool time he will have after using a Cub Cadet.

The Danco UD-6 gearbox was used on most gear drive Cub Cadets until 1980 as the only choice for a reduction gearbox. Most service parts for this gearbox are still offered, but they are getting harder to locate. It should be noted that speed shifting of the underdrive gearbox will definitely cause a reduced life of the part.

An after-market tractor parts company named M&W Gear Company of Gibson City, IL, also made a gear speed reduction unit for the Original. The M&W unit differed from the Danco in that it offered three-speed range, direct-drive, under-drive and over-drive. With the M&W model 9C gearbox installed, the tractor now had 9 speeds forward. A single lever controlled the range selection on the M&W gearbox like the Danco, but the addition of the M&W box necessitated a change to the tractor. The M&W gearbox went between the tractor's transmission reduction drive gearbox and the fabricated front frame. The cast iron gearbox was filled with 80-90W gear lube (as with the Original transmission). Brake rod extensions were supplied so that the OEM-supplied brake bands could still be used.

By moving the shifting lever all of the way forward, overdrive speeds of 3.4, 4.7 and 10.8 miles per hour would be achieved in first, second and third gears, respectively. The center position of the lever was used for under-drive speeds of .7, .9 and 2.0 miles per hour. By pulling the lever all of the way to the rear, the tractors stock speeds were engaged. Reverse speed was still the stock 2.6 miles per hour. It should be noted that it is very important the engine speed is low and the clutch pedal is fully depressed before changing the speed range lever on the nine speed. This was not like driving an old twin stick Mack truck transmission. Split shifting was not an option here and could actually lead to gearbox failure. It should also be noted that the 10.8 miles per hour top speed would require the steering gearbox, front axle, drag links, tie rod ends all be in top mechanical condition. If not, operator loss of steering and serious injury could result.

This M&W nine-speed gearbox made the tractor about 4 inches longer. A super stretched Cub Cadet, if you will. An Original equipped with an M&W gearbox is a very rare find.

M&W only made its reduction gearbox to fit the Original and discontinued it after the tractor was dropped from IH's production. Sadly, all of the blueprints for this gearbox were lost to fire in the 1990s and M&W does not service gearbox parts anymore. No production figures are known to exist that show how many gearboxes M&W made. The M&W model 9C gearbox is not adaptable to other model Cub Cadets because of design changes to the transmission housing and frame.

The Original used a single band-type brake that contacted a brake drum located on the left rear axle shaft outside of the tractors final drive. The drum was held onto the shaft with a #127 woodruff-style key. The band could be easily serviced without major disassembly to the tractor.

Cast iron rear wheel weights (each weighing 26 lbs) could be added for additional ballast if needed. IH did not recommend a maximum number of weights that could be used, but for most conditions, two weights per wheel were sufficient. The ironic story of the Cub Cadet wheel weights is that they are also the same weight used on the front wheel of the Farmall Cub and Cub Lo-Boy tractors.

The Cub Cadet Original was a basic two-color tractor that matched the IH industrial tractor line. The hood, seat, grille screen, and wheel rims were painted IH 901 white. The footrests, control knobs, handle grips and steering wheel were painted black. The rest of the tractor was painted IH 483 Federal Yellow. This trademark yellow/white paint scheme as used on all of the Cub Cadets built (except the 82 red series) in varying shade changes through the current Cub Cadet being made today. Consumers associate brand names and color schemes with

The castle in the background is actually the Catholic Diocese building in Joliet, Illinois. The 7 horsepower Original outfitted with a 42-inch front grading blade, rear wheel weights, and tires chains makes the task of snow removal heavenly. Notice the homemade toolbox at the rear of the tractor.

Not every Original was sold to suburbanites. Many found their way to farms across America performing a variety of chores. Here, an Original with a Sweepster broom sweeps the alleyway in a modern dairy farm; tomorrow it may be moving earth or mowing the yard. *State Historical Society of Wisconsin*

Cadet tractors were returned to IH after completing testing and later sold.

An optional rear mounted 3-point hitch could be added to allow the use of rear mounted implements such as disc harrow, moldboard plow, and rear grading blades. A sleeve hitch adapter was necessary to attach most of these implements to the tractor. A spring assist was available, as an optional attachment that would reduce the lifting effort needed to raise heavy rear implements. This lift assist was comprised of a heavy spring connected to the lifting linkage. When the implement lift handle was pulled back, the spring helped to lift the attachment too by compressing until the lift handle had traveled over center. The lift force needed by the operator was greatly reduced when the helper spring was installed. This lifting kit was especially necessary when using a front-mounted snow thrower or rear-mounted tine earth tiller.

Sleeve hitch implements are standard sized in their mounting hitches. This means that any sleeve hitch style implement could be used with an Original that was equipped with a sleeve hitch adapter. Also, a sleeve hitch implement that fit a Cub Cadet would also fit on a Brand X tractor provided the Brand X has a sleeve hitch attachment. Several manufactures of sleeve hitch implements made adapters to fit various brands of tractors. The adapter needed for Cub Cadets is still offered as service parts (at the time of writing this book) from Cub Cadet.

IH offered five basic factory labeled (had IH insignias on them) attachments for the Original Cub Cadet. The 42-inch wide front mounted blade was actually made in two versions. The early version is easily identified by its lack of dual

each other. Whenever a OEM tries to change from the norm it usually fails miserably. Deere learned this lesson quickly when it offered its Patio series of tractors in the late 1960s with a choice of red, yellow, blue or green hoods, seats, and trim.

The production of the Original barely kept up to its sales. In 1960 IH made 19,090 copies of the Original. IH sent 133 of these tractors to its Canadian branches and 45 to its foreign sales branches. It's interesting to note that 24 of the pre-production Cub

springs that allow the blade to trip if an immovable object was encountered. The non-spring trip blade was built in 1960 and part of 1961 only. It can be also identified by its lack of a sub-frame mounting bars that extended to the foot rests of the tractor. This blade could be angled right or left by a tube on the left side of the tractor. The 1960 production blades have a tie rod end joint attached to a threaded rod to angle the blade. The 1961 production blade used an L-shaped adjusting rod with a series of holes drilled into it that slipped inside a tube mounted to the tractors left side. By inserting a pin in the desired hole, the proper blade angle could be a made. This blade also had an unusual feature of replaceable tips, and a bolt-on snow deflector for the top of the blade. This deflector would keep snow from overflowing the top of the blade and remain in front of the blade instead. Today, this blade can be a rare attachment to find.

After several complaints and suggestions by customers, IH developed an improved version with dual trip springs and mounting sub-frame. The spring trip mounted blade was first offered in late 1961 and continued in production through 1963. IH engineers found that by adding the spring trip feature the blade would pivot forward and then up to pass over an obstruction, then return automatically to it normal position. To reduce the shock impact to the tractor, a mounting sub-frame was developed. This sub-frame helped to transfer the shock loads of the blade away from the front grille casting to the rear frame of the tractor. The sub-frame attached to the round pipe used for the rear footrest support. This blade featured replaceable cutting edges and adjustable skid

shoes, and also could be angled to the left or right at 15 or 30 degrees angle by pulling a spring-loaded pin. The lever-controlled blade has a working range of 2 inches below ground level to 8 inches above.

A two-blade, 38-inch-wide rotary mower deck was the only mowing deck offered for the Original. It also is the only deck that will fit on the Original. Later-style mower decks can be adapted to fit the Original, but major modifications are needed. The mower deck was driven by a front-mounted pulley attached to the engine crankshaft, ahead of a pulley that was connected to the starter/generator. A belt ran from the engine directly down to two idler pulleys ahead of the front axle. Here the belt twisted direction and was connected to a center-mounted double pulley on the mower deck. Another belt ran from this double pulley on the center of the deck to the right hand spindle pulley. A step-on foot operated belt tensioner pedal pulled this second belt tight by sliding the center pulley on a moveable mounting plate.

After 1961, the mounting plate's design was changed for increased durability. By stepping on the pedal, the mower was engaged. This is hardly a safe manner of mower engagement by today's safety standards, if you happen to own and/or operate older lawn power equipment please be careful during operation. Read the manuals and become completely familiar with how the machine runs. The safety features found on current machinery were most likely added because of a lawsuit or injury case that eventually mandated safety features to be upgraded.

The unique feature of the mower deck that separates it from all of the

other decks that IH offered is that there are two spindles that are connected with a cogged belt that contacts grooved pulleys on each spindle. In order for a mower deck to give a clean cut, the mower blades must overlap each other. Plainly, the blade cutting arcs must cross each other or else a thin strip of unmown grass will be left. By using a cogged belt, the spindles can be timed so that the blades do not contact each other when spinning. This allows the two blades' cutting arcs to safely overlap each other. Whenever changing blades or the cogged belt, the deck needs to be put "in time" so that the blades won't hit each other.

A dual wheel-gauge wheel attachment was offered for those who may have uneven lawns or encounter rough terrain that may cause the mower to scalp the ground. The gauge wheels could be adjusted to three different heights to match cutting height preference.

Another implement that IH offered was the model #1 two-wheeled, latch dump trailer. IH management decided that it needed to offer a dump cart that was compatible with the Original, because the trailers that were currently offered in the marketplace were crude and poorly designed. The #1 trailer was constructed of 14-gauge steel with a protective edge around its perimeter. The trailer box was watertight and could be used to mix concrete, mortar or similar materials. The capacity of the #1 trailer was 6 cubic feet or approximately a standard mixer batch of mortar. The wheel rims and tires were those used on the Cub Cadet tractor. The trailer box was purchased from an outside vendor, with IH fabricating the axle tongue and tilt latch.

Because the trailer box is angled on all sides, it not only aids in dumping, but also acts as fenders for the wheels. This angle design also eliminates the need for a rear tailgate. This trailer was handy to haul nearly anything that could be put into it, including dirt, rocks, sand, concrete, etc. The trailer also had a front mounted lever that when pulled allowed the trailer body to tip rearward for unloading. The #1 trailer was painted Harvester White and has an IH decal placed on the tongue as the only identifying mark used. Finding one of these trailers today can be quite challenging but quite rewarding to most collectors.

Danco Manufacturing built a 36-inch wide, front mounted snow thrower for the Original. This snow thrower was called the model BB-36. This attachment was driven from the tractors engine by a "V" belt, which traveled from the PTO drive clutch on the engines downward toward two idler pullies. Here the belt twisted and then went to the pulley located on the snow throwers driving gear box. Pulling a tightener rod located on the left side of the tractor tensioned this drive belt. When this lever was moved, the snow thrower's 90 degree gearbox was engaged, turning a driveshaft, which in turn moved a chain sprocket that would then rotate the combination impeller auger/blower.

To control the output of the snow thrower, a rotating blower chute could be turned 180 degrees from right to left by turning a hand crank rod that was on the operators right side. This rod had a spool on the end of it, which had a cable connected to the blower chute. The cable pulled the chute in the direction the rod was turned.

A replaceable cutting edge could be reversed to give the owner twice

IH offered a wide range of implements sized to fit the Cub Cadet. One was the #1 dump cart, shown dumping a load of fresh dirt for a landscaping job. Note the rear sleeve-hitch adapter on the tractor (shown in white) that allowed sleeve-hitch implements to be attached.

the life of the cutting edge. Two adjustable skid runners at each end of the auger housing could be used to set the scraping height of the machine. When operated in rocky or gravel conditions, it was recommend that the shoes be adjusted to their highest setting to prevent rocks from damaging the auger or becoming projectiles in the snow stream.

It's interesting to note that IH offered snow throwers for its Cub Cadets and Cadet lawn tractors not snow blowers. There is a difference between the two. A snow blower has an auger that breaks the snowdrift down and feeds the snow into a separate fan/blower wheel. A snow thrower has an auger that breaks down the snowdrift, but it also has paddles welded to the auger that expel the snow. A snow blower is typically called a two stage meaning that the snow has to be processed in two stages before it leaves the machine. A snow thrower has only a single stage to pass the snow through.

The simple four-bar spike-tooth harrow termed the model #1 peg tooth harrow also debuted with the Original in 1960. This pull-type harrow was ideal for finish grading of lawns or other landscaping projects. By moving a front-mounted lever, the operator could control the angle of all four bars of teeth for maximum or minimum penetration of the earth. The #1 peg-tooth harrow was sized to fit the Original's 7 horsepower frame. It was not a section of a larger, farm-tractor-size harrow mated to the tractor. All of the implements that IH offered for the Cub Cadet line were engineered specifically for the tractor's horsepower, traction, and physical size, And they were all painted a solid IH 901 white.

The billboard in the background tells the story of this photo. The weather in Chicago my be frightful, but using an Original with a cab enclosure and broom to move freshly fallen snow can be delightful. Then again, you could use your Original to cut grass in Florida during the winter. *State Historical Society of Wisconsin*

CHAPTER 5

EXPANDING THE CUB CADET LINE WITH HIGHER HORSEPOWER MODELS

The Original Cub Cadet was a huge success for International Harvester (IH). To retain the market share of the Cub Cadet line IH decided at the very start of the Cub Cadet production to periodically update the line as needed. In 1963 it became apparent that the single model offering was not sufficient to meet the growing need of the Cub Cadet market.

The Cub Cadet Line Grows—Again! Models 70 and 100

In 1961 when the Original Cub Cadet tractor was built, IH forecasted sales of around 5,000 units per year. Of course this estimate was extremely low as the popularity of a well-built, affordable, tractor was

IH replaced the Original Cub Cadet with the model 70 in 1963. The hood and grille styling and driveline were changed from the Original on the 70. An unusual task for a Sweepster broom is using the broom as a power lawn thatcher. The tractor appears to be doing a great job. A 7 horsepower Kohler engine powered the model 70; the rear fenders shown were optional.

In 1965, IH introduced the world's first infinitely variable speed hydrostatic-drive garden tractor, the model 123. A 12-horsepower Kohler-brand air-cooled engine powered the 123. This engine powered a Sunstrand-brand hydrostatic drive unit that was mated to the Cub Cadet differential drive housing. Here we see the business end of the 123, it is a multi-finned (for cooling) hydrostatic drive unit.

quickly accepted by the public. Production of the Cub Cadet line soared to nearly 20,000 units in its first year of production. It nearly doubled again in 1962 and 1963, with more than 65,000 Cub Cadets built by the end of 1963. IH knew it had a big money maker in its hands with the Cub Cadet line.

Initial feedback from early users of the Cub Cadet indicated the need for more power. Mowing tall grass and blading heavy soil would tend to overload the 7 horsepower engine. The V-belt drive to the clutch mechanism was one of the weak links and received complaints from users. IH engineers redesigned the Cub Cadet frame to be a twin-channel welded steel assembly. This allowed them to lower the engine in the frame for a straight-through driveline to the transmission. A new model powered

by a 10 horsepower Kohler engine was released for sale and called the 100. The 7 horsepower engine model was retained but renamed the model 70. The first number of the model indicated the engine horsepower and for the first time since the 1910s, an IH model number actually indicated the actual engine horsepower.

Both the 70 and 100 were the first Cub Cadets to have ball bearings in the front wheels. The use of sealed ball bearings offered less rolling resistance and allowed for higher front end loads to be carried.

IH retained the basic three-speed forward one speed reverse transmission from the Original for use in the 70 and 100. IH engineers made a small yet important improvement not only to the 70 and 100 and also the Cub and Cub Lo-Boy. All four share the same basic transmission and a notch was added to the shifting fork body to place additional metal at the bottom of the shifting fork lips to prevent the lips form bending. This may have been done because more and more consumers bought Cub Cadet tractors, and fewer had probably ever driven a tractor. This lack of experience often times caused clutch slippage or speed shifting the transmission. Here, the gear selector lever would be moved but the drive-clutch pedal was not depressed. This caused the transmission gears to grind loudly (the transmission does not have an internal brake to stop gear rotation). With enough force the driver would get the machine into gear, but in the process of doing so, would grind the gears against each other and the shifting fork(s) would wear, bend, or break. The latter being the most severe case. By making the forks stronger, IH engineers hoped to reduce the failure

rate and warranty claims. The huge listing of approved attachments kept growing with the 70 and 100. A totally new series of mowing decks were developed that offered a better cut on the 38 inch model, and a new 42-inch-wide cut mower deck was added. The 42-inch deck was built in response to the customer who wanted not only a more powerful tractor, but also a larger mower to match. Both the 38-inch and 42-inch mowers were built with a three-blade design. The center blade was larger than the two equal-size outer blades. A triangular shaped mower deck housing featured the center pulley offset ahead of the outer blade spindles. All three spindles featured replaceable, tapered Timken roller bearings. The spindle shaft was keyed at the top to accept a drive pulley. The use of three cast iron housings formed the basic corners of the deck and a stamped steel sheet formed the remainder of the deck housing. A scissors-type parallel linkage lift was developed to lift the frame as a level unit. An easy method to identify one of these mower decks is to look for the cast-iron end caps, also, the left side had a molded cast-iron skid shoe. The lack of a center anti-scalp roller and eyebolts mounted to ears on the cast center spindle-frame housing also are great identifiers. Both of these decks were attached to the mower-lifting sub-frame by pins; these decks were commonly known as the pin-on decks. The new decks offered a cutting height range of 1 to 5 inches.

To operate the 38- and 42-inch decks, a new front-mounted PTO clutch attachment was developed. The basic design of this clutch remained virtually unchanged until it was replaced in 1974 with an

A rare factory photo showing several Cub Cadet 123s being assembled, tested, and readied for shipment. Note the lack of front and rear wheels, which were attached by the dealer during pre-delivery, prior to sale to the customer. This assembly line process would be repeated tens of thousands of times during the production of the Cub Cadet at Lousville Works.

electro-magnetic style clutch. The PTO clutch was a straightforward mechanical type with a manual engage/disengage that could easily be removed if service was required. The clutch used a cast iron pulley that rode on a standard 1-inch sealed bearing with locking collar. The bearing was connected directly to the front of the tractor engines crankshaft (actually the clutch attaches to the rear of the engine, but because the engines are mounted with the blower fan toward the *rear* of the machine, the referencing

directions are switched). A manually operated, stamped steel control lever that had a sintered fiber button pressed into it, engaged a metal thrust button on the PTO clutch pulley. This metal thrust button had a groove machined into it that traps three-stamped steel throw out levers. This button also had a large triangular-shape metal spring that not only centered the steel button, but also helped engage the clutch with minimal lever pull effort required by the operators. These levers pulled on three

spring-loaded machine screws that either squeezed or released a steel pressure plate. When the lever squeezed the plate, the PTO is engaged (PTO is on). When the lever released the plate, the PTO is disengaged (PTO is off).

The fiber friction disc trapped between the pulley and the pressure plate serves as the wearing member in the clutch that takes the abuse and was meant to wear out. A field package service kit is offered that contains the wearing parts needed to repair the clutch. The outside of this fiber disc

This IH employee is testing the hydrostatic drive of a new 123 Cub Cadet on the assembly line prior to shipping. All Cub Cadets were subjected to a rigorous inspection process before being released for shipment. Strict quality control procedures were followed to ensure that every Cub Cadet met IH's high standards.

had a series of lugs. These lugs were shaped to fit inside the pulley cup of the separate pulley used by the starter/generator. This stamped-steel pulley is located directly behind the PTO clutch and next to the engine block. IH service manual GSS-1369 states that "The clutch will operate satisfactorily if four lugs are broken, providing the four broken lugs are not grouped together." After installing this new clutch setup on several test bench units, a rattling noise could be heard. To fix this rattle IH engineers devised anti-rattle springs. When replacing a clutch, equally space and install the three anti-rattle springs on the friction disc lugs on the non-driving side of the lugs. To understand this, if you are facing the tractor from the front, the non-drive side of the lugs is the left side. Install the springs with the flat side toward the inside of the drive hub. The rounded edge

of the springs should face toward the front of the tractor. By using these springs, the engine rattle that is sometimes mistaken for a loose pulley or bad connecting rod bearing can be eliminated.

When removing the PTO clutch from the engine for service, IH service manual GSS-1369, states to "remove the jam setscrew and lock setscrew from each of the three holes in the clutch pulley housing." Be sure to double check that all six setscrews have been removed before using a three-jaw puller or similar device (not that one is necessary to remove the clutch). The outer three setscrews have a flat cup point" on them. The inner setscrews are pointed to grab the bearing edge and retain the bearing to the clutch. When reassembling the clutch pulley to the machine, be sure to install the pointed setscrews first. Install the three locking setscrews too. This makes a

tremendous difference in the bearing and clutch pulley life. Another tip is to check the pressure plate for scoring or excessive warping. If the plate is over .010 inch it should be replaced.

An extremely important operating tip that this author has learned over the years (as an operator and as an IH dealer service manager) is that if the tractor does not have a PTO powered attachment installed, the PTO should be left in the engaged position, making sure that the mule drive belt is not installed. If the clutch is disengaged, the fiber and steel thrust buttons are contacting and wearing on each other. If a belt powered implement is not being used, the PTO should be left engaged so that the buttons are not contacting each other thereby saving a lot of premature parts wear. By following this simple tip (which is also listed in the owners manual) you can save yourself countless hours of downtime and money.

The 70 and 100 introduced a totally new method of mounting attachments to the tractor. The 42-inch-grading blade received several changes to make it more user friendly. The blade angling was improved with a choice of three angles. Angles of 10, 20, or 30-degrees, left or right, was now possible. Also, the 16-inch high blade had a curvature that was engineered to roll the load ahead of the blade. This feature produced a boiling action of the material being pushed, reducing blade rolling resistance and increasing capacity.

Two new implements were added to the line. The rear-mounted blade and rake were the newest members of the growing family of IH-approved attachments. The rear blade was 42 inches long, 10 inches high, and offered five different angle positions.

Model	Engine	Engine horsepower	Transmission Type	List Price
Original	Kohler	7	Gear	
70	Kohler	7	Gear	$690
100	Kohler	10	Gear	$765

It also could be reversed 180 degrees for backfilling operations. The 41-inch wide rake featured replaceable high-carbon steel teeth. It was interchangeable with the blade and could be angled. The rake could be used for landscaping jobs such as mulching, seedbed preparation, spreading stone or gravel or for raking leaves or debris. Both the rear blade and rear rake was adjusted manually with a spring-loaded latch holding them at the desired angle. These attachments were also raised by the attachment-lifting lever on the tractor.

A new 36-inch wide snow thrower attachment made for IH by the Danco Company cleared a 36 inch wide path, and could throw snow 20 feet, depending on snow conditions. As with the previously issued implements, these were painted a solid IH 901 white in color.

However, with only the model 70 and 100 offered for sale in 1963 through 1965, and the competition quickly growing in the garden tractor line, IH needed to change the Cub Cadet line. Marketing research by IH indicated the public was asking for (what else?) a more powerful Cub Cadet, because its uses kept expanding.

New Cub Cadets: Models 71, 102, and 122

In July 1965 IH responded by expanding the Cub Cadet line to a three tractor model series. The 7 horsepower model 70 and 10 horsepower model 100 were to be replaced by the new models 71 and 102. An all-new 12 horsepower model labeled the 122 was added to the line.

These three new models offered easier starting with the addition of an automatic compression release feature on the Kohler-built engines. This new feature as made possible by reshaping the camshaft profile so that when the engine was operated at cranking speed, the exhaust valve would stay open longer, thus allowing the electric starter-generator to crank the engine over easier. By leaving the valve open longer, the engine compression ratio was not changed dramatically, and the decreased compression resistance meant the starter/generator used less amperage to start the machine. This feature, the Automatic Compression Release (A.C.R.) was especially helpful in colder climates, or if a battery was weak. The A.C.R. disengaged when the engine rpm rose above 300. Distinguishing features associated with a Kohler A.C.R. engine were that it started quick in cold weather, there was never a kickback, it started with an easy pull (engines with recoil starting), and it never flooded from over choking. Kohler engines had A.C.R. as standard equipment on all of its single-cylinder engines above 6 horsepower since 1965.

The fuel tank capacity of the 122 was expanded to a whopping 8 quarts for extended operation. The 71 and 102 retained the previous model fuel capacities of 5 quarts and 6 1/2 quarts respectively.

A newly styled tubular steel grille (styled to simulate the grille in the IH 56 series agricultural tractors) replaced the expanded metal screen grille of previous models. A newly tooled, cast iron grille housing that incorporated smoother lines, paired with new hood sheet and product graphics, was also added. The steering pedestal and instrument panel were revised too. A new rear fender design for models 102, 122 and 123, which used flat metal fenders instead of the previous crown fenders, along with longer and wider foot rests added to the new look. New color styling gave these three Cub Cadets a totally new look of power. All were painted similar to their predecessors with black grille and foot supports. The wheels and hood retained the IH 901 white with the remainder of the tractor IH 483 Federal Yellow.

The operators comfort was not ignored with these new models either. A deluxe upholstered padded seat was added on the 102 and 122. The 71 Cub Cadet retained the previously used stamped steel seat with a C-spring suspension. The seat on the 122 and later on the 123 could be tipped forward over the steering wheel for convenience of adjustment, or to keep out rain and snow. The seat of the 102 had the same features, except it did not tilt forward. These padded seats added to operator comfort to make those long periods of operation easier. By tipping the seat forward, the operator could access a handy under-seat storage area that could be used to hold tools, gloves, etc.

The proven automotive style steering that had been used in prior model Cub Cadets was retained, with a 6.8-foot outside turning radius; sharp enough to encircle the toughest trees in your yard.

Model	Engine	Engine horsepower	Transmission Type	List Price
71	Kohler	7	Gear	$735
102	Kohler	10	Gear	$845
122	Kohler	12	Gear	$905
123	Kohler	12	Hydro	$1,082

IH eliminated the push button starting switch used on previous models and replaced it with a new key switch that had the starting position built into it. A separate push-pull lighting switch was retained from the previous models. A clutch pedal safety switch was added to all of the Cub Cadets. This switch was activated when the clutch/brake pedal was depressed. If the pedal was not depressed, the machine would not turn over.

The basic list price on the model 71 without electric starting was $660. If electric start was added, the price was $735. The 10 horsepower model 102 had a list price of $845. The 12 horsepower model 122 listed at $905. The new 12 horsepower hydrostatic drive model 123 listed at $1,082. Today, these tractors can easily bring their original list price in the collector marketplace.

The list of options a Cub Cadet owner could have equipped on their new machine grew nearly as fast as their uses. All of the options offered with the previous models were still offered. However, the addition of a charge indicator (ammeter) ($3.94 list price) and cigarette lighter ($3.25 list price) are especially handy for cell phone users that have power adapters today, were offered for all models. An implement lift helper spring was available to ease the lifting of heavy implements.

IH offered a huge selection of special equipment and accessories for the new Cub Cadet owner. Original list price for a 38-inch rotary mower was $139; 42-inch rotary mower was $156.

By updating the Cub Cadet line, IH was able to keep its 23 percent market share of the garden tractor market, the largest of any garden tractor manufacture. This was a highly profitable market that IH was not about to give up to anyone. But, IH had a new idea that was soon to be unleashed on the competition that would change the industry forever. An idea that every competitor in the market would eventually copy from IH. It was called the hydrostatic transmission or hydro for short.

The Hydrostatic Drive Transmission Is Added

The use of hydrostatic transmissions has been around for quite some time; the aircraft industry uses this method of power transmission for systems on airplanes. IH started to experiment with hydrostatic (hydro) transmissions in 1959 by installing English built Lucas hydrostatic transmission and radial drive motors in an IH 340 utility tractor that was renamed the H-340 (Hydro 340). This tractor was a huge engineering success. But IH engineers decided to have some fun" with the H-340. They installed a 90 horsepower Solar (a wholly owned division of IH) turbine engine to replace the 4-cylinder C-135 IH gasoline engine. A tractor of this type really needed to stand out from all of the rest, and after some futuristic hood and rear platform restyling, the HT-340 (Hydrostatic Turbine), turbine-powered hydrostatic-drive tractor was born. It looked part tractor and part rocket ship and it was both. IH exhibited the HT-340 everywhere it could. Starting in 1961 the HT-340 was exhibited at many farm shows and other IH-sponsored events. Eventually the uniqueness of the HT-340 started to wear off, and it was in need of some general maintenance. The mass production feasibility of a turbine powered farm tractor was very dim. The HT-340 was quite loud and was not very fuel-efficient. Yet, a hydrostatic drive tractor showed great potential.

IH was growing tired of showing the HT-340, as it had served its experimental purpose—to put a hydrostatic-drive transmission in a farm tractor. IH contemplated selling the HT-340 at auction, but later decided to donate it to the Smithsonian Institute in Washington, D.C., for permanent display and care.

This was a milestone advancement not only in tractor farming technology, but for IH too. Hydrostatic drive models would soon dominate the Cub Cadet line and nearly every competitive line of garden tractors.

IH unveiled the first ever production farm tractor with a hydrostatic transmission in 1967 with the IH 656 Hydrostatic tractor. IH assembled their own hydrostatic-drive farm tractor transmissions in what was called the white room at the Farmall Works. This was state-of-the-art, climate-controlled room provided a dirt- and dust-free environment which was absolutely critical for correct hydro assembly.

What made a hydro so unique from other methods of power transmission used in farm tractors? In one word—smoothness. Smooth operating both in accelerating and decelerating, and infinitely variable speeds. The operator always had the right speed for the job, never having a gear that was too fast or too slow for the job. No clutch to adjust, replace, or wear out. These new hydro drive tractors were ideal for PTO and shuttle direction work. Exactly the kind of work that a Cub Cadet did a lot.

In the fall of 1965 the model 123 hydrostatic drive Cub Cadet was unveiled. This totally new drive system once again proved IH the leader in garden tractor technology. The use of the new infinitely variable, entirely clutchless hydrostatic transmission was especially helpful in landscaping, snow removal and mowing operations. The hydrostatic transmission didn't have a belt to slip and pulleys to move like the variable speed transmissions found on other brands, nor did it have gears to shift or grind and clash.

A variable displacement hydrostatic pump transfers mechanical energy (rotating of the driveshaft from the engine) into hydraulic energy (compressed oil). This is then channeled to the fixed displacement hydrostatic motor which converts the hydraulic energy (compressed oil) back to mechanical energy (output of final drive gears).

Because pressurized oil was pumped to a hydraulic motor which in turn moved the drive tires, power train slip was negligible (fluids are not compressible) and power transmission was super smooth.

The speed and direction of travel were controlled by the displacement of the hydrostatic pump. Because the rate of fluid flow, direction of fluid flow and pressure are all three infinitely variable, infinite speeds are possible.

The hydro unit acted as a drive train shock absorber when being used to change direction or to accelerate and decelerate because of the fluid coupling effect of the hydrostatic transmission. One of the drawbacks of the hydro was its inability to transmit engine torque to the driving wheels. Also, the hydrostatic pump/motor unit required that at least a 10 horsepower engine be used as the tractor's power plant. The extra energy was needed to pump oil in transmission and was basically lost in this process.

IH used a direct drive shaft to the hydrostatic transmission from the engine, similar to the gear-driven models. No wimpy belts or chains were used here. A single dashboard-mounted SR (speed-ratio) lever controlled both the direction and speed of travel. As the operator moved the SR lever forward from the neutral location, the Cub Cadet increased in forward travel speed. If the lever were pulled back toward neutral, the forward travel speed smoothly decreased. Reverse travel operated in the same manner. It was as easy to operate as "1-2-3." Is this how the model number was devised? Who knows. By depressing the combination clutch and brake pedal with the operators left foot, the hydrostatic transmission was returned to neutral with the pedal fully depressed; this was a built in safety feature.

The Sunstrand Company of Rockford, IL, manufactured the hydrostatic drive pump/motor unit. Sundstrand would continue to be the exclusive hydro supplier to IH and later, Cub Cadet Corporation (CCC). (Sundstrand would also market similar versions of this hydro to other OEM's for their line of lawn and garden tractors.)

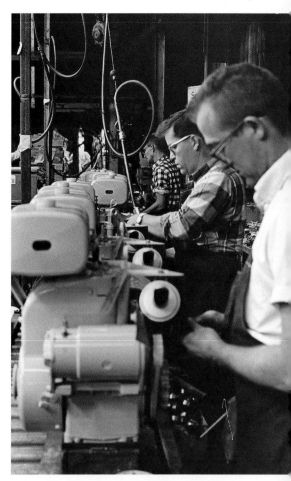

Before the engine goes in, the parts go on. In this photo, Kohler engines destined for various Cub Cadet tractors ranging from 7 to 12 horsepower are being trimmed. The front PTO, muffler, and related parts are added prior to assembly of the tractor.

This hydrostatic pump/motor was coupled to the rugged final drive housing used on the gear driven Cub Cadets. The rear end housing not only acted as a structural member, (such as on the gear driven Cub Cadets) but also served as the reservoir for the hydraulic oil with an oil capacity of 7 quarts. This basic hydro/final drive housing design lasted until 1998 when the garden tractors were built by Modern Tool and Die Company (MTD) and, in this author's opinion economized. Ironically, in 2001, MTD brought back the cast iron rear

The 1968 IH lineup of power lawn products is shown here. With machines ranging in size from the model 60 (6-horsepower rear-engine rider) to the 10-horsepower gear-drive model 104 and the 12-horsepoewer hydrostatic drive model 125. IH even offered a 15 horsepower version of the Cub Lo-Boy, which it later renamed the 154 Cub Lo-Boy. IH used blue accenting striping in this series.

differential housing. Almost every major competitor of Cub Cadet used Sunstrand hydrostatics in their units.

Because hydraulic oil was used to deliver power in a hydrostatic drive, and fluids are not compressible, high oil operating temperatures will occur, from the oil being constantly being compressed and pumped to move the tractor. Unless the oil is cooled, oil viscosity breakdown will occur and the oil

will fail. On larger agricultural tractors, a separate hydraulic oil cooler (radiator-type device) is used to cool the hydraulic oil, (Case-Ingersoll, an IH competitor used this type of cooling on their lawn and garden units) however, due to the compact size of the Cub Cadet, an innovative alternative was devised. Metal fins (such as those found on the Kohler air-cooled engine powering the Cub Cadet) were cast on

the hydro pump housing. A drive-shaft-mounted four-blade fan would draw clean, cool air from underneath the center of the tractor and blow it back over the hydro unit, exiting the rear of the tractor. The original fan was white cast aluminum. A tubular guard was placed around the fan to protect it from damage. Later, a screen was added to the opening on the frame to keep debris out and avoid overheating the hydro. A sheet-metal air deflector was installed directly behind the hydro pump/motor under the seat. This deflector directed air to the lower side of the hydro for even cooling.

A single spin-on, full flow, throwaway hydraulic filter was used to keep the hydraulic oil clean. This was easily changed from the underside of the tractor with-out removing panels or disassembling the tractor. The filter used on the original 123 hydro has been updated internally over time, but it still had the same basic mounting threads and sealing ring as the current filter sold today. It is important to note that not all oil filters can be used to replace the hydraulic filter. Many engine lubricating oil filters have a much coarser filtering media inside them. Even though they may filter out particles down to 3-microns, a hydraulic oil filter has a media rated at 10 microns and can trap much finer particles. Also, engine oil filters may have an added filter bypass valve. This bypass valve allows oil to bypass the filter if the filter becomes clogged. The very fine machining tolerances of the hydrostatic pump and motor require clean filtered oil. If unfiltered oil is used in the system, serious damage and/or failure may occur to the pump/motor. Be sure to ask for and use only genuine OEM (Original Equipment Manufacturers) approved hydraulic oil filters for your Cub Cadet. The extra cost—if only a dollar or two—is well worth it when you can eliminate the problems that other will fit filters will cause.

The oil used in the Cub Cadet hydros, Hy-Tran, was the same hydraulic oil IH used in its agricultural tractors.

Over the years, IH constantly updated Hy-Tran with new additives to make it better. Today, the original Hy-Tran hydraulic oil has been updated to Hy-Tran Ultra and its compatibility with other oils, water absorption, and corrosion-inhibiting qualities have been greatly improved. Hy-Tran can absorb up to 3 percent of its volume in water. This is especially important for those whom use Cub Cadets for snow removal in colder climates. Typically when operated in colder climates, the oil is heated during use, and then cools when parked. While the oil cools, water vapor tends to accumulate in the transmission/differential housing.

Because there is not a water drain-off valve, it is important to regularly service the hydrostatic transmission. Change the oil and filter at the same time. A helpful hint when doing this is to remove most of the bolts holding the rear differential cover. Place a large catch pan (at least 2-gallon) under the rear of the tractor. *Slowly* pry the cover away from the housing. A large gush of oil will follow. After the oil has drained, remove the remaining bolts and wipe the inside of the cover clean. Replace the gasket with a new one part #350837R3. Spray the inside of the housing with brake cleaner to remove any sludge build up. The sludge that is found at the bottom of the housing is actually Hy-Tran that has absorbed all of the water that it can and it has precipitated at the bottom. Also spray the bolt holes in the rear casting with brake cleaner and wipe dry with a cotton swab. Be sure the housing is dry inside and re-attach the rear cover. *Do not* use silicone, RTV sealant or any other gasket eliminator type of material in place of or on the gasket. Install the gasket dry. One of the hardest parts of servicing the Hydro is adding oil to the rear end. IH used a pipe plug in the rear cover as both the oil level check and fill hole.

A flexible funnel or suction gun works best to refill the machine with oil. It was only after the sale of the Cub Cadet line to Modern Tool and Die Company (MTD) that an oil fill tube and dipstick become part of the machine. After filling with oil, drive the Cub Cadet and operate the Hydraulic lift (if equipped) to help circulate the oil. The system is self-bleeding, meaning there is no need to open any valves to let air escape. Stop the machine, turn off the engine, and recheck the oil level. All Cub Cadet hydrostatics hold seven quarts of oil.

The most common problem associated with hydros is called hydro creep. This is when the SR lever is in the neutral position or the brake/clutch pedal is depressed, and the tractor either creeps forward or backward very slowly. To correct this, do the following: Raise the tractor so its left rear wheel is off the ground. Start and run the engine at half throttle or faster. Move the SR lever to the forward speed position. The wheel should rotate forward. Depress the pedal fully and then release the pedal. The SR lever should return to neutral and the wheel should stop turning. If the wheel does not stop, check to see if the SR lever has the proper friction adjustment. To check the lever friction adjustment use a fish or other small scale to measure the pounds of pull when the lever is moved in either direction. The desired amount of pull should be 10 pounds. If the lever tension is correct, the connecting rod going from the S-R lever to the speed control cam needs to be adjusted. If the rear-wheel creeps forward, turn the rod counterclockwise to lengthen it until the wheel stops. If the creep is in the reverse direction, turn the rod clockwise to shorten it.

The uses for a hydrostatic-drive Cub Cadet were nearly endless, almost like the lifetime of the Cub Cadet itself. The durability of a hydrostatic drive was improved over the years, but it should be noted that lack of maintenance or improper use (towing with a car or truck) caused most hydro failures. The hydrostatic helped IH Cub Cadet sales increase immeasurably through the years. Later, in the mid 1970s, IH would expand its use of hydraulic technology in the Cub Cadet line to operate the attachment lift and even remotely powered hydraulic cylinders on Cub Cadets. Two years after the introduction of the 123 Cub Cadet hydro, IH would use the hydrostatic drive transmission technology in the IH 656 agricultural tractor. The popularity of the 123 is evident by its 16,318 units being made by IH in its brief two-year production run. The first production model 123 was serial number 157,490. IH also heavily advertised the 123 as being simple to operate. Simple as 1-2-3.

The 123 hydro optional equipment and styling were the same as those offered on the model 122 Cub Cadet, and was the 12 horsepower gear drive equivalent to the 123.

IH painted the hood, seat rails, and wheel rims IH 901 white. The foot supports and front grille screen were painted black, and the rest of the tractor was painted IH 483 Federal Yellow. Model identification decals on the Cub Cadet 123 resembled a royal crown. The blue and silver colors of the decal looked very sharp against the IH 901 white painted hood. Maybe this was intentional by IH, but in the years to follow, hydrostatics would be king!

Within 10 years, every other competitor would use hydrostatic drive in their tractors. This is another example of IH being the true leader in lawn and garden tractor power.

The International 1 Rotary Tiller

In March, 1966 IH released to its dealers the International 1 Rotary Tiller. This rear-mounted attachment required the tractor be equipped with a 3-point hitch, and preferably a spring lift assist too. Instead of developing a complex rear PTO drive system or using the existing transmission PTO drive (which turns the wrong direction for PTO powered implements) IH engineers made due with what they had and built around it. Most Cub Cadets were sold with the standard front PTO clutch attachment. By using this and a modified mower deck drive system, the rotary tiller could be located at the rear end of the tractor but be powered by the front end. The two idler pullies used on the mower-deck mule drive were kept, but a long V-belt ran to the rear of the tractor where it engaged a pulley on a 90 degree gearbox (the same gearbox used to power the front mounted snow thrower attachment).

This gearbox had pullies on both shafts with the output shaft connected to the rotary tiller attachment with a V drive belt. The rotary tiller attached to a bracket, which also mounted the 90-degree gearbox to the differential rear cover. When the rotary tiller is attached to the tractor, the rear drawbar was removed. The rotary tiller that IH sold was painted IH 901 white and was manufactured for IH by Danuser Machine Works of Claremore, OK. The tiller has three decals on it. Two decals were caution/warning instructions, the other was simply International. As with the International #1 dump cart, the International #1 rotary tiller does not have a 1 decal on it.

Sales of the International #1 rotary tiller allowed IH to finally penetrate the home garden market that had been previously ruled by walk behind units made by other manufactures. This tiller also saw extensive sales to landscape contractors who had already been using the Cub Cadet system.

Quick Attachment for Cub Cadet Models 72, 104, 124, and 125

In Tractor Committee Report # 232 dated May 1967 IH proposed to replace the current model 71, 102, 122, and 123 Cub Cadets with new, improved models. The models 72, 104, 124, and 125. These new models, according to an IH report, would have new styling that consisted of "a new cast-iron grille housing with lines to blend into and coincide with the lines of the fenders and the steering pedestal." A new, easy to remove grille insert was also included. The use of red and white trim on the hood and instrument panel and a new seat would make these new Cub Cadets more pleasing in appearance. A new molded fiberglass instrument panel that fit into the hood for better appearance also was added. The instrument panel was made wider and deeper, and included a center dash mounted ammeter. The lift lever was chrome plated and had a new float latching mechanism. This feature would allow the mower deck, front blade, or snow blower to float over the contours of the ground.

The new models were the 7 horsepower gear-drive model 72, the 10 horsepower gear-drive model 104, the 10 horsepower hydrostatic drive 105, the 12 horsepower gear-drive model 124 and the 12 horsepower hydrostatic-drive model 125. IH built three prototypes of each model for various purposes. One of each model was built for testing and photographic use. The other two were built for display at the National Hardware Show held in October 1967. These tractors would be displayed with a sampling of typical implements including the new 38-, 42- and 48-inch mower decks. Production of these new tractors was slated to start in November 1967.

Tractor Committee Report #236 dated 8-3-1967 stated the reasoning behind the new additional model Cub Cadet, the 105 hydrostatic. It stated that "The committee has closely watched with gratifying interest the reception given to the introduction of the hydrostatic drive 12 horsepower Cub Cadet 123 last fall, of which 5,962 units have been delivered to users as of July 22, 1697. This, plus the highly satisfactory functional and structural performance, together with the enthusiastic dealer and customer acceptance of this model, has not only proven its marketability but has resulted in new market appraisal. The committee now believes it would be profitable to expand the line of Cub Cadet tractors by the addition of a hydrostatic-drive 10-horsepower-size tractor." It also states that "The proposed additional model will utilize the same hydrostatic transmission and controls as the new 125 model, and the same engine as the new 104 model. It can best be visualized as being the same as the new 125 hydrostatic-drive model except for the engine size (10 horsepower instead of 12 horsepower) and rear tire size (same as 10 horse-power gear drive) and with a new model designation."

Therefore, the 105 was a hybrid tractor of sorts. Part 10 horsepower gear drive part 12 horsepower hydro blended together to make a new model. IH and other OEM's used this

The best way to get the consumers attention is to put your product in front of them. IH teamed with Kraft and its Miracle Whip-brand salad dressing to give away 25 trips to Hawaii, 125 hydrostatic-drive Cub Cadet tractors, and 140 other prizes. This in-store display was a sure-fire way to get the consumers attention. There are 384 jars of Miracle Whip in the IH #2 trailer if anyone was counting!

method of borrowing parts from several tractors to make a new model size they needed. It is a low-cost method of product engineering. Production of the 105 was slated to begin in November 1967.

The basic hood and grille shape of these new Cub Cadets was nearly identical to the previous models. The footrests were now painted black, not yellow, and all models have a distinctive blue striping the entire length of the hood and instrument cowling. The upper grille panel and lower grille screen were the new parts added to these models.

Even the largest yards were quickly conquered with the IH Cadet 1X8/1X9 series tractors, which were styled to match the IH 66 series farm tractors.

The hydrostatic-powered models had a new one-piece die-cast lever to enhance its appearance. This lever replaced the simple curved metal rod handle that was on the 123. The lever still was pushed ahead to move forward, and pulled back for reverse. A neutral location was between the two directions.

All of these new Cub Cadets still were painted in the familiar yellow/white combination paint scheme, but the IH white paint was changed from the #901 to a new color #902. The IH 483 Federal Yellow paint color remained unchanged. IH would continue to use #902 IH white until 1971 with the new models 73, 106, 107, 126, 127, and 147 tractors.

The tractor frame had been modified to accept the quick-attach mounting of front and center implements without the use of hand tools. Two jaws under the front grille casting accepted the mounting bar attached to the implement. A special shoulder bolt on each side of the tractor frame, located behind the front axle, formed an anchoring point for attachments. A special spring-loaded latching bar had been added for changing implements. By squeezing this bar, the sub frame could be pushed on to the tractor frame.

A toolbox had been added to the seat support on the 10 and 12 horsepower models for operator convenience. Also, rubber insulation pads were added to the hood for isolating

Model	Engine	Engine horsepower	Transmission Type	List Price
72	Kohler	7	Gear	$777
104	Kohler	10	Gear	$915
105	Kohler	10	Hydro	$1,070
124	Kohler	12	Gear	$995
125	Kohler	12	Hydro	$1,150

vibration noise. Two latches were added to positively latch the hood to the steering pedestal.

A new line of quick-attach implements also was announced to match these new models. They were front-mounted blades, center-mounted mowers, and a new front-mounted snow blower. The new mower decks were easy to install and remove without the need for tools. A 38-inch, 42-inch and a whopping 48-inch wide cut decks. A threaded eyebolt was used to adjust belt tension, with the ideal setup having the two front idler pullies parallel in their distance from the front of the mower undercarriage support. All three decks used the time-proven IH deck-drive system of a mule-drive belt which extended down from the PTO clutch mounted on the front of the engine, to two spring-loaded idler pulleys, and then to the center double pulley on the deck. Below the mule-belt center-drive deck pulley was the deck drive belt. This belt turned all three blades on the deck and featured an automatically adjusting spring loaded belt tensioner. On the 48-inch deck, a special spindle drive system was used. Each spindle from left to right, was driven progressively faster to help discharge cut material and allow faster mowing speeds. This new drive system was studied on the 38- and 42-inch decks for their performance in possible future revisions.

These new decks were easily identified by the lack of cast-iron mower-deck spindle housings on the outer spindles when compared to the previous model decks. The deck shell is of a heavier gauge stamped-steel design than the previous model mowers, with only a cast-iron front nosepiece used. These heavier-gauge deck shells were implemented to conform to new safety requirements of the American Safety Association. The spindle bearings were still a tapered roller and separate seals design, and could be serviced individually if necessary. The 48-inch deck featured an attachable safety shield that was required to conform to new ASA safety standards.

These new model mowers began production in November 1967. IH painted all three decks similarly; the deck housing was IH 902 white and the belt shields were IH 483 Federal Yellow. The serial number of the 38-inch decks had a 381U prefix on the serial number plate; the 42 inch had a 421U prefix; and the 48-inch deck had a 481U on the plate.

These new mowers and related lift linkages were designed so that new mowers could be used on older model tractors as replacement decks for worn original equipment. They also offered the improvement of quick-attach of the mower lift linkage for easy mower cleaning and servicing. The new lifting linkage also permitted a Cub Cadet owner to use a new tractor with

their old mower, even though this greatly reduced the benefit of the quick attachment. The combination of a new tractor and a new mower would have been the best choice to offer the operator ease of changing attachments whether it be mower, front blade, or snow thrower. Any attachment that was mounted by the rear 3-point hitch or sleeve hitch would still fit on these tractors. IH replaced the International #1 trailer in 1967 with its new model International Cadet #2 trailer. In Tractor Committee Report #235 dated 7-19-1967, this decision was approved. The International #1 trailer had been in production since 1960 and had fair sales reception by customers. Objections to the trailer's lack of ability to be fully dumped from the tractor seat were its main complaint. To change this, IH proposed to sell a new trailer that was designed to be fully dumped from the tractor seat. The square design of the trailer with a removable end gate and built-in stake pockets meant adding sideboards could be easily accomplished for increased hauling capacity of light bulky loads. The full-dumping feature of this trailer is made possible by rotating the trailer body around the axle. This also added the feature of being able to store the trailer in a vertical position which required minimal floor space.

IH decided to purchase a five-year inventory of the trailer form Ohio Steel Fabricators in Columbus, Ohio. If preliminary sales projections were met, the trailer could be fabricated at the Louisville Works at a later date. The International Cadet #2 trailer had a list price of $82.50 compared to the $92 list price of the old International #1 trailer. The International Cadet #2 trailer was painted entirely IH 902 white.

CHAPTER 6

A NEW LOOK FOR THE CLASSIC CUB CADET

On February 3, 1969 the International Harvester (IH) Farm Equipment Division Tractor Committee held a meeting to propose an improved lineup of Cub Cadets. Tractor Product Committee report #278 tells of these improvements. It states that these tractors would have revised functional features and new styling to maintain and enhance the IH position in the garden tractor market. This tune-up was "necessary to combat the activity occurring in this area by major competitors which would adversely affect IH's sale-ability of the present popular IH Cub Cadet Line.

The plans called for the replacement of the model 7 horsepower model 72 Cub Cadet with an 8 horsepower model (model number unknown). This plan was based on the anticipated introduction of a 7 horsepower-mowing tractor (later to be called the Cadet 76) concurrently with the new model 107,

Relaxing on the patio with a cool glass of lemonade is possible with the new 14-horsepower hydrostatic-drive 147 Cub Cadet. A hydraulic lift makes the 48 inch mower deck raise at a fingertip touch. Notice the yellow deck roller and the lack of a mule-drive belt to the mower deck.

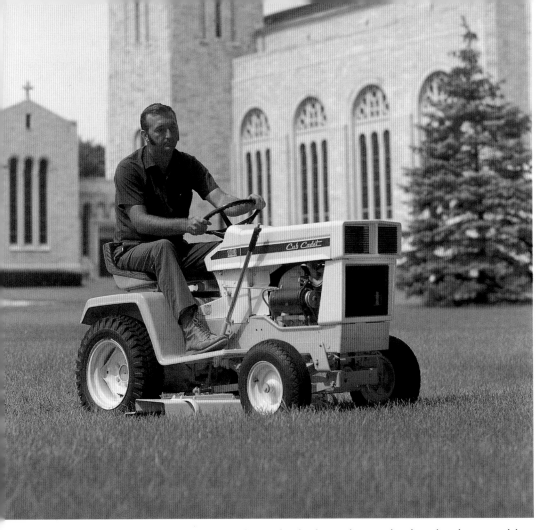

The green stripe on the hood and the hydro dump valve decal are indications that this Cub Cadet is a model 109. The 1X8 and 1X9 series Cub Cadets were the first models to have the starter/generators painted black.

126, and 127 Cub Cadets in 1970. However due to the necessity of utilizing available engineering manpower on higher priority programs, (farm tractors and combines) the 8 horsepower model would not materialize at this time. Thus, the model 72 would be replaced with the Model 83, but was later renumbered as the Model 73. This involved a change of decal only.

IH needed to remain competitive in the 7-horsepower-size market, and they could do so by retaining this model. The 106 would replace the model 104, the 107 would replace the 105, the 126 would replace the 124, and the 127 would replace the model 125 from the former product model line.

The pride in owning a Cub Cadet tractor had reached a point where many repeat sales were being made on the premise of owners wanting to have the newest models, even if their current machines had many remaining hours or even years of life left in them. This was quickly becoming a driving force in the repeat sales of Cub Cadets. It was therefore recognized that the line should be updated every two years or so, especially since competitors like Simplicity, Deere and Bolens had introduced similar updated models to the market.

These new models would gain a new, attractive appearance by the use of a new hood with new lines added to its design. The hood could be raised to service the engine and fuel tank, and is latched to the pedestal by spring-loaded sliding pawls. A new instrument panel and cowling was designed to add eye appeal and blend in with the hood. A totally new one-piece sheet-metal stamped rear fender was used to eliminate the seams, weld spots, and

This studio photo of the Cub Cadet model 86 tractor is clearly a prototype, indicated by the "86" that has been laid over the decal stripe as a separate piece. IH often used prototype units in its literature so that brochures would be ready when machine production started. Because prototypes were used, many times they differed slightly from the actual production unit.

hardware; it also added to the new stylish look. This new rear fender design gave the Cub Cadets added eye appeal. Its wider design affords more tire coverage, and larger foot rests. A new dual spring suspended seat with backrest offered added operator comfort as well as contributed to the new look of the Cub Cadets. Arm rests were also made available as factory or field installed attachments too.

The PTO lever had been relocated to the left side. The new chrome-plated tube handle with spring loaded latching mechanism offered a functional improvement as well as a styling improvement. The use of two-wheel disc brakes on the 10 horsepower and 12 horsepower models were standard equipment with a rubber pad on the pedal for improved appearance. IH engineers evaluated the addition of a limited-slip differential to be either a factory-installed attachment as standard equipment or field installed by a dealer. It was never built as the cost of incorporating this feature was not conducive to IH remaining price competitive in the marketplace.

The basic three speed forward one speed reverse transmission was carried over from the previous series to be used on the new gear-drive models in this series. The hydrostatic transmission was also retained. A small yet important change occurred to the hydrostatic model at serial number 281800. IH engineers added a small brace to the hydro suction tube to stabilize the tube from vibration and pulsation. Field failures were not rampant on this issue but it was an important item to fix to retain loyal customer.

Electric starting was provided on all models. The demand for hand start had been insufficient to warrant

Model	Engine	Engine horsepower	Transmission Type	List Price
73	Kohler	7	Gear	
106	Kohler	10	Gear	$1,065
107	Kohler	10	Hydro	$1,230
126	Kohler	12	Gear	$1,155
127	Kohler	12	Hydro	$1,320
147	Kohler	14	Hydro	$1,545

Keeping your yard in perfect shape is easy with the 147 and its 48 inch mower deck. Special care should always be taken when operating near obstacles, such as this rock retaining wall. With the tulips in bloom, yard care season is just begining.

The model 59 grinder/shredder takes the hard work out of yard work! By using a Cub Cadet, leaves and yard waste can be quickly ground into useful compost. The Cub Cadet tractor powers this attachment via a belt from the engine PTO.

The model 149 with a powerful 14-horsepower Kohler engine, hydrostatic drive, and hydraulic lift will help any homeowner keep their yard in picture-perfect shape. The standard equipment of front headlights help get yard work done.

retention of this option. This is another example of how IH was able react to the consumers needs in positive ways.

One prototype was built in October 1968 to achieve the latest styling as recommended by the Farm Equipment Division Tractor Committee for their approval. Four additional prototypes were built for additional engineering testing, sales announcements, photographic purposes (literature), with the provision of production retooling. Since the majority of the changes was styling for these new models, re-testing of the engine or power train was unnecessary because these components remain unchanged. IH planned to replace this series of Cub Cadets in the fall of 1971.

The production numbers of the 106 totaled 16,635 units. The 107 totaled 10,846 units. The 126 totaled 5,247 units. The 127 had 25,485 units made. From these production numbers it's easy to see that the hydrostatic-equipped tractors outsold the gear-drive-equipped tractors approximately 2:1.

It is unique to this series of tractors that they were painted IH 902 white and were painted two different colors of yellow. The earlier built tractors up to serial number 335967 were painted the old IH 483 Federal Yellow. Tractors serial number 335968 and after were painted the new IH 483B Federal Yellow. It is possible to have two original painted tractors (a 127 for example) that are two different shades of Federal Yellow in color and yet still be correct.

IH was busy making changes to its mower decks for added reliability. One area that received a fair amount of engineering was the spindle bearings. IH engineers spent many hours researching and testing new bearings. At first, a new style automotive-type bearing was used. This was a

IH's first entry into the low-cost "Lawn Tractor" market was the 7-horsepower model 76 Cadet. The 32-inch-wide mower deck was ideally sized to yards that were too big for a walk-behind, but too small for a Cub Cadet Garden tractor. The Briggs & Stratton 7-horsepower engine powered a three-speed Peerless-brand transmission via a V-belt drive.

one-piece design fitted into stamped steel flanges. This new bearing (ST721) was used on the 38 and 42 inch decks. A larger-capacity bearing (ST722) was used only on the 48 inch decks. These bearings still used the internal threads that accepted a bolt and washer to retain the spindle pulley to the spindle.

The 14 Horsepower Model 147 Hydrostatic

The Farm Equipment Division Tractor Committee Report #292 dated 6-27-1969, released the most powerful Cub Cadet to date, the new model 147 Hydrostatic drive 14 horsepower Cub Cadet.

IH realized the need for a more Powerful Cub Cadet as there had been a definite indication of acceptance of offering a 14 horsepower lawn and garden tractor. This tractor would meet the needs of higher power and performance requirements in applications such as heavy grass mowing or heavy snow removal operations. The need for this model was such that it would help IH meet the growing consumer needs for a more powerful model and to ensure that IH would maintain and enhance its advantageous position in a very competitive marketplace.

The 147 had a hydrostatic drive transmission to fully utilize the available engine horsepower. The Kohler 14 horsepower engine had features such as: exhaust valve rotators, stellite exhaust valves (for longer life), and the engine was balanced to minimize vibration.

The term "engine balancing" was not something new; high performance racing engines are balanced. By doing this, high speed vibrations are reduced or eliminated for better engine performance, and less vibration is transferred to the machine and ultimately the operator. In short, balanced engines run smoother. To accomplish this, Kohler used a set of offset weighted gears that were driven by the engine crankshaft. At high speeds, these gears absorbed crankshaft vibration and the engine lunge was less noticeable at higher speeds.

Electric lift was standard equipment as was two front headlights and two rear taillights. To operate the electric implement lift, the operator simply moved a dash-mounted switch, offering fingertip lifting of any

To celebrate the United State's bicentennial, IH built a specially painted version of the 76 lawn tractor appropriately called "The Sprirt of 76 Cadet" in the years 1975-1976. The distinctive red, white, and blue paint scheme is shown here with 20-year-old Charlene Zimmerman of Ottawa, Illinos. This tractor has become very collectible, with few original models left.

attachment without the need for spring assist or a strong arm. This lifting feature could be easily added to the 106, 107, 126, and 127 models. The frame was modified to accept the wider engine blower housing, but matched the rest of the 1970 line of the Cub Cadet tractors in appearance and styling.

An increased-capacity front PTO clutch was standard equipment on the 147. This was necessary to handle the increased engine horsepower that was being generated. The increased capacity PTO clutch had two friction discs to handle the increased engine horsepower being transmitted.

Two experimental models were built by IH. One model successfully completed the PTO clutch cycle testing, and the other was employed mainly in field testing of mowing and hydrostatic transmission testing to ensure compatibility with the 14 horsepower engine. The 147's were also painted in IH 483 and 483B Federal Yellow with IH 902 white. The serial number of the first production 147 is 316816. During its three-year production life IH made 15,678 copies of the 147, sent 110 units to its Canadian branches and 20 units to its foreign branches for retail sales.

Cub Cadets Tenth Anniversary

The year 1971 marked the Cub Cadet's tenth birthday. IH did not build a special tenth anniversary edition, but it did remember the birthday of its fastest growing product line.

This is a true story as told by Don McAllister of IH: A man bought a Cadillac and a Cub Cadet on the same day. His neighbors came over to see—you guessed it—the Cub Cadet. This was just a typical example of how garden tractors have captured the public eye.

Model	Engine	Engine horsepower	Transmission Type	List Price
86	Kohler	8	Gear	$1,147
108	Kohler	10	Gear	$1,249
109	Kohler	10	Hydro	$1,441
128	Kohler	12	Gear	$1,351
129	Kohler	12	Hydro	$1,450
149	Kohler	14	Hydro	$1,799
169	Kohler	16	Hydro	$1,799

The Cub Cadet was originally designed for industrial use, and it was built heavy. This heavy-duty design tended to influence the long life span of the machine. Even in 1971, a full 10 years after the Cub Cadet Original hit the farmsteads, fairways and factories of America, many were still going strong. An IH official was quoted as saying "Many Cub Cadets are operated by women and by men who are not mechanics, so the Cub Cadet line has to be reliable. It has to be easy to operate and easy to maintain, changing attachments has to be simple. That's the way we designed the Cub Cadet". And, "The Cub Cadet has prestige. It has tremendous image, and people take pride in owning a Cub Cadet. . .The popularity of the Cub Cadet has been gratifying, and we expect that popularity to continue". Some very truthful words for a little tractor that literally had taken America by storm, opening a whole new market of sales opportunity for IH.

In 1977, IH added the hydrostatic-drive Cadet 80 lawn tractor to its lineup. A homeowner is shown towing a #2 IH sweeper. The big 9-cubic-foot capacity is making the job of collecting leaves seem almost effortless and is a big time saver.

With a 16-horsepower Kohler engine under the hood and hydrostatic drive, the 1650 Cub Cadet was the largest model in the new Quiet Line series of tractors. Special rubber engine mounts, side panel enclosures, and larger mufflers made these tractors quieter and more comfortable to drive.

The Wide-Frame Cub Cadets

International decided to make a change to the Cub Cadet lineup in 1971. The frame was widened from 11 to 14 inches. This also meant a new lineup of attachments had to be developed to fit these new wide-frame models. Was the saying "wider is better" really applicable here as it is in a game of golf or auto racing? Yes. IH realized that higher horsepower Cub Cadets were going to be needed to meet future consumer needs. These higher-horsepower models would transfer more stress to the frame and adding extra gussets or increasing the gauge of steel would not be the answer. These new higher horsepower engines had wider engine-blower fan housings and needed more room to mount directly to the frame.

In September 1971 IH released the new lineup of wide frame Cub Cadets. These were the models 86 8 horse-power three speed gear drive; 108 10 horsepower three speed gear drive; 109 10 horsepower hydrostatic drive; 128 12 horsepower three speed gear drive; 129 12 horsepower Hydrostatic drive; 149 14 horsepower hydrostatic drive; and later, in 1974, the most powerful Cub Cadet built to date, the 16 horsepower hydrostatic drive model 169 Cub Cadet. Once again, the first one or two digits indicated engine horsepower, an odd-number suffix indicated hydrostatic drive, and an even number indicated gear drive.

Again, IH marketing found that it needed to update the Cub Cadet line to keep their market share from eroding to the competition. It had been three years since the addition of the big 14 horsepower model 147, even though the 149 was the current 14 horsepower model, and the line needed to be beefed up. Adding a new 16 horsepower hydrostatic model 169 was the IH way to accomplish this.

While these Cub Cadets were still painted in a familiar IH 935 White (after serial number 375939) and IH 483B yellow scheme, a number of improvements lurked under the newly styled hood and front grille. A massive cast-iron front grille support was still used, but now recessed square pockets were used to locate the headlights. Directly below this was a black die cast plastic grille. This entire front casting/grille loosely resembled the new IH 66-series agricultural tractors grille introduced at the same time.

The battery was relocated away from the engine compartment to a new location under the operator's seat. By moving the battery away from the heat and vibration of the engine, longer battery life could be achieved. Easier battery access for routine maintenance could be achieved by simply tipping the operator seat forward. The extra weight of the battery over the tractor's rear axle also aided in traction under slippery conditions.

Now that the battery was removed from the engine area, the fuel tank was moved back away from the engine

This studio shot of a 1250 Cub Cadet is shown with a 44-inch mower deck attached. The lever-operated implement lift could be equipped with a spring assist to help in lifting heavy implements. The use of an electric PTO clutch on the engine meant that flipping a switch would turn the mower on or off.

closer to the dash. This helped to keep the fuel cooler and help prevent gasoline vapor lock. The fuel tank capacity was increased to 2 gallons on all the models, while the previous series offered the 2-gallon size in only the 126, 127, and the 147. Also, by moving the tank rearward, the chances of spilled fuel or an overfilled tank igniting on a hot engine were reduced. (Never refuel ANY fossil fuel powered machine until the engine has cooled off. Many serious injuries and even deaths have occurred by not following the suggestions in the owner's manual. Follow the safety suggestions in the manual.)

Kohler engines made a change to the cylinder head design of the 12 and 14 horsepower engines it produced for IH. The major change was the relocation of the spark plug for better

combustion. The spark plug was moved towards the valve openings, away from the cylinder bore. Because the cylinder head had a new hole pattern, the sheet-metal heat baffle covering the top of the engine was changed to accommodate this. These new engine changes occurred at tractor serial number 438962.

The manually engaged front-engine-mounted implement PTO clutch was retained from previous models, and the chrome-plated PTO control lever was still on the left side of the steering pedestal. Changes were on the horizon for the safety of lawn power operators. IH service bulletin #S-2462 dated 12-18-1972 announced a number of changes to the PTO clutches of the Cub Cadets including the change of the PTO lever and handle

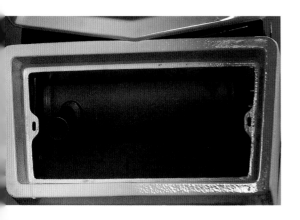

Here's a key part in making the new Quiet Line tractors quiet. A large-diameter muffler toned down engine noise; the front exit pipe pushed engine noise, heat, and smoke away from the operator; and special shielding directed engine heat out the front of the tractor.

assemblies to accommodate use of the either single or dual-spring PTO repair kits and single or dual-disc repair kits. These new controls were added at serial number 392192.

A new dual-disk, dual-spring clutch assembly also was released for use on the 106, 107, 126, 127, 147, and the 86-149 series tractors. These kits could only be used if the aforementioned lever and handle kits were installed, and was available for service parts and factory installation after 9-13-1972.

A new clutch pulley that would accept either style of clutch kit was offered staring with serial #400015. Finally, a PTO safety starting switch was added to the 86-149 series tractors after serial number 441194, to comply with new safety standards. IH already had previously only used a safety switch on the clutch/brake pedal. The machine would not crank over unless the pedal is depressed. Tractors equipped with the PTO safety-starting switch could not be started unless the PTO was disengaged. Likewise as a mechanical PTO operating tip, the tractor should not be operated for long periods of time with the PTO disengaged in order to prevent premature wear/failure of the fiber wear button. All model 169 tractors had the new PTO safety switch installed. This new safety switch also meant that the wring harness had to be modified to accept the new circuitry. Only the new style harness (part #56286C91) would be offered as a service part for both the early and late production machines. On the earlier-built machines, a short wire that connected both contacts would be installed for proper function.

A new, hydraulic attachment lift was optional for the 109 and 129 and standard on the 149 and 169. Instead

A **54**-inch front-mounted grading blade could be attached to a Quiet Line tractor, as shown, to make grading earth or gravel a fast and smooth job. Optional front hydraulic outlets on the models 1250, 1450, and 1650 equipped with hydraulic lift could also be used to power a blade-angling cylinder.

of using an externally mounted reservoir/pump assembly, the 1X9 series had a higher rated pressure in the hydrostatic transmission charge pump. This extra pressure was needed as the lifting cylinder derived its hydraulic lifting power from this pump. The cylinder moved the implement lifting rockshaft and had a provision to lock out the float feature of the lift mechanism. The chrome-plated hydraulic lift control lever was on the right side of the dash console. The basic instrumentation and operating control layout remained the same from the previous models. An electric lifting option, that was available as a field installation on

the gear drive models, was offered as optional equipment on the 109 and 129 after serial number 400,001.

The use of a combination starter/generator was still employed throughout this series, although this would be the last Cub Cadet series to use this starting method. The starter/generators were painted black. These were bought directly from Delco and were installed on the tractor after it was painted. Also, an electric attachment lift could still be ordered as optional equipment on the 86, 108, 109, 128, and 129 Cub Cadets. This was operated by a dash-mounted toggle switch that activated an electric screw drive motor. This lifting method

In an obviously staged photo, a Cub Cadet 1200 with a 42 inch front blade is shown pushing "snow." The light, fluffy "white stuff" was no match for the 1200's 12 horsepower engine and three-speed transmission.

worked well in colder temperatures where the hydraulic lift may have been sluggish at times (cold oil has a high viscosity). Electric lighting was also an option for all of the aforementioned models and came as standard equipment on the 149 and 169 for those requiring illumination of the dark. An ampere gauge centrally located on the dash kept the operator informed of the electrical systems performance.

Adjustments and Attachments

Vehicle safety was becoming an important issue for IH, as more consumers were using outdoor power products, including many machinery-challenged individuals. IH realized this and incorporated a braking feature into the front PTO clutch after serial number 482,000. This would not allow the PTO-powered attachment to coast to a stop or continue to

operate after the PTO was disengaged. This style of clutch is easily identified by two large metal discs (one stationary, one rotating), with fiber material epoxied to each. By using a combination brake shoe/engagement pin disc, the PTO could be positively stopped in seconds. In an emergency situation, seconds can make the difference between life and death. Unfortunately these new safety features were created as a response to accidents that had already occurred in the lawn power equipment industry on all makes of machines.

One of the oddest pieces (and actually the rarest in this authors opinion) attachment ever made by IH, for the Cub Cadet line was its protective canopy, first introduced in 1973. The combination of the Cub Cadet's lower center of gravity matched with this new protective frame offered a level of driver protection that had not yet been available. The rugged 2- by 1-inch 11-gauge tubular steel frame was securely bolted to the tractor frame. This new safety canopy offered three benefits to the Cub Cadet owner. The frame protected the driver in case of a tractor upset or rollover, and protection from low hanging tree limbs that they may not see. A yellow and white vinyl-coated duck top measuring 24 by 32 inches helped to shade the operator and offered some protection if the rain started before the mowing was done (it also featured an attractive white fringe).

The frame stood 72 inches from the ground. Two important components that helped to complete this package were a seat belt and a pair of rear-mounted steel skid bars used to protect against rear overturns. To find this protective canopy today can be quite a challenge. These are considered very rare in the collector world and often command a premium price when—or actually if—they are found.

In the spring of 1973, IH made several improvements to their line of mowing decks for several reasons. One important change was the addition of mower deflectors to all three sizes of mower decks that IH offered. The 38-inch, 42-inch, and 48-inch mower housings were all changed to

accept the new deflector. This change was necessary to comply with newly introduced mower safety standards. All decks after serial number 1113 have the new deflector installed on them. The purpose of these new deflectors was to keep any foreign material from exiting the mower rapidly and acting as a projectile, causing damage or injury. IH engineering also was busy fine-tuning the mower deck spindles again, in advance of its new series of decks that it was designing. The main improvement to the deck spindles was the replacement of the old-style spindle bearings with a new spindle that had external threads on the upper end. The spindle pulley was now retained by jam nuts instead of a bolt and washer. These new bearings are part numbers ST745 for the 38 and 42-inch decks, and ST746 bearing used only on the 48-inch deck.

Two totally new mower decks, known as the model 44 (44 inch cut) and model 50 (50 inch cut), replaced the older model 42- and 48-inch mower decks. While still retaining the easy quick-attach mounting system, these two new decks offered greater parts commonality with more than 95 percent of their parts.

These new mower decks were to be used on Cub Cadets serial number 400,001 and up. They are quick detachable by the use of two, spring-loaded handles and two bayonet-type hangers on the front deck. The two bayonet hangers fit into a pair of cast eyebolts that can be used to level the deck fore to aft.

Using a one-piece stamped-steel housing, the 44 and 50 decks used three water pump-style spindle bearings (ST-745). These bearings were re-greased through a zerk at the

Dual hydraulic control levers on the model 1650 made your Cub Cadet more useful. The outer lever controlled implement raising and lowering; the inner lever operated the optional front hydraulic outlets. All of this control is right at your fingertips with a Cub Cadet.

top of their shafts. All three zerks were accessible without removing the deck. The parallel lift linkage allowed the deck to be adjusted in height from 1 to 4 inches depending on tire and mower combination. The prior model 48 and 42 decks had a few units made with a similar deck bearing setup, but they used a ST 742 bearing instead

A mule-drive belt tension release lever at the front of the tractor offered a dual purpose. It not only served as a tension release lever to allow the mule belt to be changed, it indicated when the belt need to be adjusted. Two V grooves cut into the lever corresponded to an indicator decal on the front of the mower undercarriage showing initial belt adjustment, and when the belt needs to be adjusted or replaced.

An enclosed-deck belt drive was featured on both the 44 and 50 decks.

A full vinyl cab enclosure and front-mounted snow thrower made quick work of clearing the "white stuff" even if the "snow" was fake. This studio photo shows a Quiet Line tractor outfitted with rear wheel weights, and tire chains for extra traction. Look at that "snow" fly!

Because all three blades are powered by a common belt, if one of the blades hit an obstruction, the other two would turn independently. This cover not only kept grass and other debris out of the belt, but also served as a stylish safety guard to keep the operator from being belt whipped, or from causing a severe foot injury. One of the drawbacks to this totally enclosed-deck belt drive was that the belt-idler pivot bolt tended to get corroded and rusted in place, usually snapping the deck drive belt when it was engaged. After Cub Cadet Corporation (CCC) took over the Cub Cadet line from IH, a grease zerk was added to the pivot bolt so the bolt could be lubricated, thus extending belt life. Using three equal size blades for each deck increased parts commonality for IH and its

dealers. The deck shells and mower blades are the only parts that are sized differently between the two sizes of decks.

The model 149 had as standard equipment a hydraulic attachment lift. A lockout pin in the lifting linkage allowed the operator to use equipment in a fixed-locked position where down pressure was required, as with a front-mounted blade or snow thrower. When a mower was attached, the lockout pin would be put in its storage position to allow the mower to float over any obstructions. An adjustable cam stop located by the operator's right footrest could be used to limit lifting handle movement to a pre-set depth.

For those who needed to use rear-mounted equipment, (such as a rotary

tiller, disc harrow, or moldboard plow) an optional 3-point hitch was available for all models. And a creeper drive attachment was offered for the 86, 108, and 128 gear-drive models.

In 1971, IH offered a new style of front-mounted snow throwers, models QA36A and QA42A. These two machines were basically identical except for their cutting width, and are often confused with their predecessors, the QA36 and QA42. While they are both QA (Quick Attachable), and still either 36 or 42 inches in width, they now have another unique feature, adjustable width or A. Thus, a QA42A were both wide and narrow frame quick-attach-style Cub Cadets. (A pretty neat engineering feature for a low-volume tractor attachment.) By having an adjustable feature, IH instantly made a new snow thrower available for older tractors. IH engineers accomplished the adjustable width feature by having the two front mounting frames made with two sets of mounting holes. When the snow thrower was assembled, either the wide frame or narrow frame mounting holes could be selected. IH sold over 2,300 copies of the QA36A in 1971, compared to 1,326 of the QA36 snow thrower. Likewise, the QA42A outsold the QA42, with 3,400 units sold compared to 1,782, respectively. The QA36A and QA42A were the only two mounted attachments that IH offered that would fit both narrow- and wide-frame Cub Cadets.

Also in 1971, IH added to its attachment lineup a rear-mounted landscape rake. This was referred to as the 41-inch rear rake. This rake used 28 spring steel, replaceable rake tines to provide the raking action. The teeth could be removed to allow a greater spacing between them, if needed.

The heart of the IH Cub Cadet is its rugged transmission/differential that was borrowed from the famous Cub tractor. Here, the gears that compose this assembly are shown in a special cut away model 1200.

The rake attached to the tractor via the rear 3-point hitch. Dual caster gauge wheels could adjust the working depth of the rake. A pair of lifting springs attachments aided in raising the rake. This rake could be used for final seedbed preparation for yards, or a rake used to remove yard wastes.

One of the most interesting attachments that IH ever offered for a Cub Cadet appeared in the 1973 attachment lineup. This was the model 59M shredder-grinder. This attachment was a front-mounted hopper with 24 reversible, swinging flail hammers that were driven via the front PTO in the tractor. The models built in 1973 and 1974 used a sliding belt-tensioning bar to engage or disengage the shredder. After the 1974 production, IH changed this to a sliding belt tensioner pulley. Similar to that found on the 44 and 50 mower decks. IH also changed the intake hopper and main frame sheets after 1974 for increased life.

This shredder could eat small brush, leaves, even pop cans, and leave and grind them as shredded bits in seconds as well as grind limbs up to 1 1/2 inches in diameter. For the homeowner who had a compost pile, or just needed to do some woodland, or leaf cleanup, the 59M made quick work of an otherwise time-consuming job. Imagine, not having to rake yard waste, or leaves, and instead just grind them to bits! Full-face protection and the use of gloves were a must with this attachment. Also be absolutely sure that the engine has been turned off and has come to a *complete stop* before trying to unclog the shredder.

Even large mowing jobs are cut down to size when a 44-inch mower and a 1450 are used. Picture-perfect results are the outcome of using this combination. Automotive-type steering allows the 1450 to handle with ease.

In 1971 IH rolled out its biggest Cub Cadet with the new 16 horsepower model 169 hydrostatic. This tractor was styled to match the other 1X8 and 1X9 series in appearance. A Kohler model K-341 single cylinder, 16 horsepower, air cooled engine powered it. The muffler used on the 169 was uniquely different from the other Cub Cadets in the 1X8 and 1X9 series in both size and physical shape. The X refers to the middle digit of the tractor model. All tractors in this series have a model number that starts with a 1 and ends with either an 8 or 9. The middle digit varies depending on the model, thus the generic "X" reference. Instead of having a 90-degree pipe elbow connecting the muffler to the engine block, an S pipe was used. All of the 169s built had the front PTO style that incorporated the disc brake feature in its design.

Hydraulic lift was also standard equipment, as was an electric powered maintenance meter. This meter was actually an electric time clock that operated when the key was on. It would record the engines running time (unless the key was left on overnight) and allow the operator to perform basic maintenance on a timely manner.

Dual front-mounted headlights were standard equipment on the 169. The 169 enjoyed a short two-year production run with only 4,005 units being built, which certainly qualifies the 169 as one of the lowest production Cub Cadets made. Also, none of the 169s were shipped to any of IH's foreign branches. The serial number of the first 169 built was 506737.

Pre-Quietline Tractors

IH was busy incorporating features that would be found in its next generation of Cub Cadet in the 1X9/1X8 series. In August of 1973 IH

Model	Engine	Engine horsepower	Transmission Type	List Price
800	Kohler	8	Gear	$1,565
1000	Kohler	10	Gear	$1,690
1100	Briggs	11	Gear	$1,790
1200	Kohler	12	Gear	$2,350
1250	Kohler	12	Hydro	$2,450
1450	Kohler	14	Hydro	$2,935
1650	Kohler	16	Hydro	$3,120

offered a noise suppression package. This package consisted of a new, larger muffler, exhaust fitting, new air cleaner and heat baffles. By installing this package, engine noise levels would be reduced over the previously specified exhaust system levels. The tractors which had the noise suppression kit installed are easily identified by their larger engine muffler, which has a 5-inch diameter compared to the previous 3-inch diameter. Also, the exhaust outlet is fitted off center of the muffler, where the old style is centered on the end cap of the muffler.

The use of a black model stripe with a thin colored pinstripe above it on the side of the hood helps to identify the model. The 86 had a gold or yellow colored pinstripe, the 108 and 109 had a green pinstripe, the 128, 129 and 169 had a red stripe, and the 149 a blue stripe. Even if the numbers are worn off of the stripe, their colored pinstripe identifies which model of the 1X8, 1X9 series that you have.

IH builds the 500,000th Cub Cadet

In early December 1973, the IH-owned Louisville Works produced the 500,000th Cub Cadet, a model 149. As with IH's 5 millionth agricultural tractor built on February 1, 1974, the 149s were dressed up in appearance. However, instead of sporting a radical paint scheme and loads of chrome accents (like the 5 millionth

tractor), the 149 simply had chrome IH hubcap wheel covers added. In the months following production of the 500,000th Cub Cadet, it toured the United States at various trade shows touting not only the features of the Cub Cadet line, but also that IH was the first garden tractor manufacture to reach the 500,000th mark and its historical significance. IH kept the 149 after its good will tour and placed it on display at its famed Harvester Farm display in the Chicago Museum of Science and Industry. After IH's sale of its agricultural division to Tenneco in 1985, the museum farm was dismantled and its contents hauled to Racine, WI. This historic 149 is still in existence and is believed to be currently owned and stored by the IH Agricultural Equipment Groups merger partner, the Case New Holland Corporation in Racine, WI.

The 76 and Spirit of 76 Cadet Lawn Tractors

In 1972, IH released an all-new machine referred to in Tractor Committee Report #278 as a mowing tractor. This was called the model 76 Cadet. The Cadet tractor series were not the same as the Cub Cadet. The Cadet line was built as IH's answer to the new market of smaller yard owners who did not need the "big" Cub Cadet but still wanted a quality product to do the job. Also, ever-increasing pressure

brought to the marketplace by other mass merchants and box stores to sell economy priced and featured lawn equipment led IH to develop this new model referred to as a lawn tractor.

The 76 Cadet was not a Cub Cadet like its bigger brothers, but had an all-new design by using a vertical crankshaft engine and belt drive to the transmission, in contrast to the horizontal crankshaft and driveshaft drive to the transmission of the bigger Cub Cadets. A stamped-steel frame and its physical size (about one-third smaller in size) helped to distinguish a Cadet from a Cub Cadet. A tilting, one-piece, fiberglass hood/grille such as those found on the IH 4200 and 4300 semi-truck tractors, opened easily to allow for engine maintenance and refueling. A Peerless brand three-speed gear drive trans-axle along with manual attachment lift and a manually operated belt driven PTO help keep the frills on the 76 Cadet to a minimum. A recoil or electric starting 7 horsepower Briggs & Stratton engine was available, however an electric lighting package was not offered. Like its big brother Cub Cadets, the 76 Cadet offered a whole range of attachments for its user including a 38-inch wide cut, below-deck mounted mower deck, rear-mounted grass bagger, a 36-inch-wide front-mounted single stage snow blower, or a 36-inch-wide front-mounted, manually angling grader blade, to name a few.

The Cadet line of tractors was not outfitted with a rear hitching/lifting system. IH built these machines to mow grass, not plow dirt. The bigger and beefier Cub Cadet was built for those chores.

In 1975 and 1976 a special edition 76 Cadet called the Spirit of 76 was built by IH to commemorate the

Several manufactures offered allied attachments for the Cub Cadet tractor line. A 1650 is shown doing garden cultivation with a Brinly-brand sleeve-hitchmounted cultivator. This adapter allows any sleeve-hitch implement to fit on a Cub Cadet. The multiple digging teeth of the cultivator could be adapted to fit a variety of row spacing.

bicentennial (200th) year of the United States. IH outfitted these Spirit of 76 Cadets with a unique paint scheme of IH red, IH 935 white and IH blue colors. The tilting fiberglass hood, steering wheel, seat, wheel rims and fenders were all painted IH 935 white. The rear fenders had IH blue stars on them, as did the top of the hood.

An IH blue colored stripe adorned the sides of the hood and wrapped over the top of the hood near the dash. Thin IH red pin striping also matched the blue hood stripes. The word Spirit of 76 was printed on the rear top of the hood in IH red. The grille of the Sprit of 76 Cadet had red, white and blue striping in the areas where headlights

could have been someday installed, along with white stars. The engine and basic chassis were IH red.

To find one of the 3,504 Spirit of 76 Cadets today can be quite a challenge. Many have been repaired and the original parts have been replaced. The hardest original issued parts to find for these are the steering wheel, (which is molded in white plastic, not black as all the replacements are), the seat, which is has a white vinyl covering and white painted metal backing, and the Spirit of 76 decal set. All of these parts are no longer available (NLA). But, these models are quickly becoming a favorite among Cub Cadet collectors and are as popular as the Original model Cub Cadet or the 169 in collectibility.

Getting Quiet, The Quiet Line of Cub Cadets

October of 1974 brought the introduction of a totally new look to the Cub Cadet line. The new line still retained the familiar IH yellow and white paint scheme, but now the engine was completely enclosed. What was the reason for this? To add an industrial designers dream to a lawn and garden tractor? A really cheap buy on sheet steel from U.S. Steel?? Actually the reason behind these newly styled Cub Cadets was IH's attempt to meet proposed noise level emission laws pertaining to lawn mowers and lawn tractors. The City of Chicago and the Federal Government had proposed these laws, and IH took them very seriously. IH was not going to have to reverse engineer the Cub Cadet line to meet these proposed laws when the line could be engineered to meet the laws right from the start.

How was IH going to accomplish lower noise levels? One idea was to slow the mower blade tip speed down. This lowered the noise from the mower deck, but the slow speed mower didn't cut grass very well, at all.

Why not concentrate on the engine noise? This is the prime noise generator on any piece of power equipment. The IH Truck division had excelled in this area quite well and the Cub Cadet engineering department adapted a few ideas from them. One source of noise is engine vibration. In the IH motor truck line the use of rubber engine mounts to deaden vibration worked great, why not use them here? Instead of bolting the engine directly to the frame as in previous models, two engine-mounting rails were employed along with specially designed rubber mounts called ISO-Mounts.

ISO Mounts were hard rubber washers with steel bushings in them. IH also used these in the agricultural tractor line to reduce vibration in the tractor cabs of the IH 66 series tractors. Now the Cub Cadet owner would not feel the vibration from the engine, because it would be absorbed by the ISO-Mounts. With the engine vibration problem solved, the engine noise emission levels could now be addressed. Working through Purdue University, and with Kohler Engines, an engine enclosure design was developed which helped IH meet the challenge. The use of side engine enclosure panels helped to direct both the engine noise and heat away from the operator by having it exit the front of the machine. Newer, larger diameter (over twice the size of the previous muffler) lower-tone mufflers were developed that helped to further reduce engine noise. IH engineers routed the engine's exhaust noise and heat out the front of the tractor, away from the operator. The previous

A Cub Cadet 1650 teamed with a Brinly-moldboard plow makes garden work go quickly no matter how big it is. To attach the Brinly plow to the 1650, a special sleeve-hitch adapter was required.

models used a side exit engine muffler, which would allow the engine noise, heat, etc. To wrap back around to the operator. The resulting lineup of Cub Cadets was dubbed the Quiet Line.

However, before the lineup was ready for production, the proposed noise emission laws were dropped. While engineering for these noise reducing features may have cost IH millions of dollars in wasted research and development costs, IH decided to keep these new features and offered a new, higher level of comfort that had never been experienced in any garden tractor of any make before. When the 1000 series Quiet Line of new Cub Cadets was announced to

the dealers and public, it caused a lot of *noise*. The kind that comes from great enthusiasm and great sales. Everyone was talking about it. IH dealers' swore by these quiet new Cub Cadets, the competition could only swear at them. But just a few short years later, most of the competitive brands also adopted the use of engine side panels to direct the cooling air, engine heat and noise away from the operator and larger engine mufflers just as IH had developed. This style of design can still be seen today in most of the lawn and garden tractors built. Just another example of IH being the true leader in lawn and garden power equipment.

Fingertip control of the hydrostatic-drive tractor is possible by a dash-mounted lever. This Speed-Ratio (SR) lever controls not only the speed of the tractor, but also the direction of travel. When the clutch/brake pedal is depressed, the SR lever returns to the neutral position.

The members of the new Quiet Line included the model 1650 Hydro 16 horsepower, the models 1450 14 horsepower and 1250 12 horsepower hydrostatic models were also joined by the models 1000 10 horsepower, and 1200 12 horsepower and 800 8 horsepower gear-driven models. Later, the model 1100 11 horsepower gear drive was added as a price fighting alternative to battle with competitive-branded "no frills" garden tractors. The 1100 had the ISO-Mount engine mounts like the other Quiet Line Cub Cadets,

but the engine side panels were not included.

The model 800 was in the Cub Cadet lineup for only two years, 1974 and 1975. IH dropped it after then and replaced it with the new model 81 Cadet lawn tractor. The reasoning behind this was simple, the 800 was overbuilt and overpriced when compared to the big box stores mowers. It was too much tractor for the market. The new model 81 Cadet was more of a direct match to the competition.

IH announced that after July 4, 1975 all of its Cub cadets would carry a full one-year warranty. This warranty would provide that IH repair or replace any part or parts that were defective in material or workmanship for the first year of ownership. The warranty covered not only the cost of the parts, but also the labor to install them at an authorized IH dealer. Any items replaced under warranty were covered for an additional 90 days or the remainder of the original one-year warranty period. Tires were not covered by this warranty because they were warranted by their own manufacture. Also, normal maintenance items such as tune-ups, oil changes, lubricants and adjustments were not covered. A one- or two-year warranty extension could be purchased at an additional cost during the original first year of warranty. Customers also could schedule a free tune-up at the end of the warranty with their authorized IH dealer.

For those who were commercial operators of IH lawn power products they could have opted to buy IH's 24-month total service maintenance agreement. For a nominal fee, IH would cover all repairs, parts and labor, and all maintenance for eligible units, except tires and batteries. Only

IH Outdoor Power Products dealers that met stringent Certified Service Standards, could perform these tasks. This service agreement called for the customer to regularly lubricate and maintain proper engine oil levels as shown in the owners/operators manuals. The customer must also contact the IH dealer to schedule periodic maintenance according to the book. This service agreement replaced any/all IH warranties if the unit was used in commercial purposes.

These new Quiet Line models also were the first Cub Cadets to use an electric-powered front engine PTO clutch. This allowed smooth PTO engagement by the operator and was easily engaged by moving a simple toggle switch mounted on the dash. A big change from the older mechanical clutch designs that required periodic maintenance and adjustment. Also, the use of a starter/generator on the engine was dropped from the previous models and replaced by a positive drive starter and flywheel-mounted stator-alternator. To help aid in starting, the automatic compression release feature used on previous models was still built into the Kohler cast-iron block engines. This allowed them to turn over with less starter power.

The hood still lifted forward for routine engine maintenance, cleaning, and for refueling. The engine side panels were retained on the side of the steering cowling by a single thumbscrew. A spring over the top of the engine held the front of the panels in place. These new engine side enclosure panels were easily removed by unlatching a spring at the front and turning a thumbscrew near the side of the dash. The entire engine compartment could then be cleaned or service could be performed.

The 2-gallon fuel tank was a new polyurethane design (replacing the welded metal) with a larger filler neck and built-in fuel level gauge. The early version of the Quiet Line tractors had the same size tank opening as the previous 1X9 series.

An expanded metal screen was used in the lower grille area replacing the solid die cast plastic grille used in previous models. This allowed greater amounts of heat and air to exit away from the engine compartment. Because nearly all of the heat from the engine was expelled through the front grille area, the plastic grille probably would have had a meltdown occur. A funny (but not to IH) problem that IH had with the new screen grilles, was that the engine air was deflected downward in front of the tractor. This was fine except that if you wanted to use a pull-type lawn rake or sweeper, the engine air blast would scatter the leaves, grass, debris etc. out of the way, making their pickup difficult. A service bulletin was issued that stated to correct this problem, a new grille screen could be ordered. The cast plastic IH emblems in the upper grille area tended to warp after being used for extended periods of time while being exposed to a partial blast of the engines heat.

Another small yet important change to the grille was the replacement of the grille hold-down springs with machine screws. It seems that the springs would unhook, allow the grille to fall out and be run over. This change occurred at serial number 565131.

The model 1450 and 1650 offered a hydraulic attachment lift as standard equipment. They also optionally offered another IH and industry first, a front auxiliary hydraulic outlet that could be used to

This studio photo shows the short-lived model 800. Powered by an 8-horsepower Kohler engine, the 800 was built from 1974 to 1976 only. The 800s were overpriced compared to lower-priced lawn tractor models in its horsepower class. Today, the model 800 is a very collectible Cub Cadet tractor.

hydraulically angle the optional front-mounted blade attachment or power small hydraulic cylinders. Two levers (inside lever used for raising and lowering of attachment, and outside lever used for front hydraulic valve control) located on the right side of the dashboard console put all this hydraulic control right at the operators' fingertips.

Another IH and industry first was the use of a tractor hour-meter. IH called it the Maintenance Minder. This dashboard-mounted meter would keep track of how long the engine runs. Its hands indicated when it was time for routine maintenance

such as filter and oil changes, so you never had to worry about missing periodic maintenance.

Later-production Quiet Line tractors saw the front wheel spindle size increased from 3/4 inch diameter to a full 1 inch diameter in size. This change took place at serial number 632502. It allowed bigger front mounted blades, snow blowers, and other equipment to be used without overloading the front wheels.

More than 50 optional attachments ranging from front-mounted brush chippers to rear-mounted PTO-driven rotary tillers helped the Quiet Line of Cub Cadets do any job, in any season.

CHAPTER 7

RETURN TO RED— THE IH 82 SERIES CUB CADETS

In 1979 International Harvester (IH) announced a totally new look for the Cub Cadet line, the color was changed from the familiar Cadet yellow to IH tractor Red. This new IH 82 series Cub Cadet simulated the look of the bigger IH agricultural tractor lineup. More specifically, they were a combination of the IH 86 series (decal striping and IH white trim) and the yet-unannounced IH 50 series (body side panels and basic grille shell design) agricultural tractors.

The reason to change colors to IH red was stated by IH "so now styling and paint complement our complete tractor line." This gave the 82 series Cub Cadets a "new look of power." The forward airflow that had been first used in the Cub Cadet Quiet Line series, and still used in the 82 series, was later adapted to the full size IH 50 and 30 series agricultural tractors, in a slightly modified form.

Powered by a smooth-running, three-cylinder, liquid-cooled Kubota diesel engine, the 782 Diesel was the first of its kind for Cub Cadet. Highly sought after by collectors and homeowners yet today, the 782 Diesel was known for its high fuel efficiency. It is easily spotted by its large external muffler on the right side.

Before you can cut the grass, you need to lay it. In this case a hard-working 682 Cub Cadet with a rear-mounted tiller creates the perfect yard. A 17 horsepower model 782, teamed with an International cart, takes the hard work out of yard work.

For those who had smaller yards, the Cadet Lawn Tractor series fit every need. The 382 Cadet gear-driven lawn tractor with its 36-inch wide cut deck made any size mowing job go quickly. The 382 also was offered in a hydrostatic-drive version.

Many new features and innovations were added to the Cub Cadet line. The engines were still fully enclosed for better sound control, and engine cooling airflow was increased. The engine choices were expanded to offer the consumer the choice of Kohler, Onan, or Briggs & Stratton power to fit their needs. The use of rubber ISO Mounts to absorb the engine vibrations had mostly been discontinued, and the engines were now directly mounted to the frame. The use of twin cylinder engines in the larger Cub Cadets greatly decreased engine vibration, and the need for the ISO Mounts.

The model 482 still retained the ISO Mount engine mounting system; the single cylinder engine required the use of this to keep vibrations to a minimum. However, it was improved with two side rails connected with cross bars to form an engine cradle. Many of the Quiet Line tractors that have had catastrophic ISO Mount and engine rail failures have been upgraded to the cradle style.

IH did not favor the use of Kohler brand engines as standard issue on

The Cub Cadet 1282 was equipped with a 12-horsepower single-cylinder Kohler engine and featured a hydrostatic-drive transmission. A 38, 44, or 50 inch deck could be matched to this tractor with over 25 other Cub Cadet-approved attachments to tackle any job.

the 82 series over other engine makes. The 982 used a twin-cylinder Onan engine as its powerplant; the 682 and 782 were equipped with KT-17 series I twin-cylinder engines; the 582 used a twin-cylinder Briggs & Stratton engine; the 482 had a single-cylinder Briggs & Stratton engine. The Kohler engines were built with a cast aluminum block with cast iron cylinder

sleeves for long wear. The Briggs & Stratton twin-cylinder engine was of a cast aluminum block construction.

Like the previous series, both gear-driven and hydrostatic-drive transmissions were offered. IH 82 series Cub Cadets were offered with either a manual or hydraulic power attachment lift. Power steering and power brakes were not offered.

The increased use of safety interlock switches was unveiled in the 82 series. A switch on the operators' seat and on the clutch/brake pedal both had to be activated to allow the machine to be started. On the Garden tractors, (models 482, 582, 682, 782, 982, 1282) when the PTO was engaged, if the operator left the seat for any reason the engine would turn off, unless the PTO had been shut off already, or the brake pedal was latched into the engaged position. Also on the Hydrostatic drive model if the machine were shifted to reverse, the PTO would turn off, but the engine would continue to run. A new electric PTO clutch with a convenient dash-mounted toggle switch included a built-in brake to stop the mower operation in four seconds. This could be a major inconvenience for those who had small, tight yards with a lot of backing required. These safety interlock switches are still used today by every lawn and garden tractor manufacturer to help prevent fatal accidents and reduce their product liability risk. These safety systems can be eliminated, but this author does not condone such action. Numerous switches, relays, and sensors had now replaced the simple electrical wiring found on the older model Cub Cadets. The wiring diagrams were actually becoming complex with all of the added electrical switches, relays and other devices used.

The model 782 had as standard equipment, four IH labeled, chrome wheel covers to really dress this model up. These chrome wheel caps also would fit the models 482, 582, 582 special, 682, and 1282 for those Cub Cadet owners who wanted to show their IH pride.

A new, professionally styled plastic instrument panel dash, which had hot stamped lettering, replaced the prior fiberglass cowling and dash decal. The wide, flat surface made viewing the ampere and Maintenance Minder gauges very easy. Also, the hydro control lever, adjustable speed control stop, throttle lever, and electric PTO switch were easily found by the operator. IH relocated the

All of the new 82-series Cub Cadet garden tractors featured a 4-gallon polyurethane gas tank that could be refilled without opening the hood. A handy gauge built into the cap indicated at a glance when it was time to refuel.

hydraulic lift and front outlet control levers to the left side of the dash, allowing the operator to use their right hand to control the SR lever and left hand for hydraulic operations. On the previous Quiet Line models, the operator needed three right hands to change speed/direction and operate the hydraulics.

The fuel tank capacity was increased to 4 gallons. That is a 100 percent increase over the previous capacity of the Quiet Line. The engines were also designed to run efficiently on unleaded gasoline.

The new larger fuel tank could now be filled without raising the hood, and a larger easy-to-read fuel level gauge was added. The tank was still made of a lightweight, rust-proof, poly material.

The chassis had many improvements too. The use of 1 inch diameter pre-lubricated and sealed front wheel bearings over the previous 3/4-inch diameter bearings and the use of a drilled bolt with castle nut for the axle pivot pin, helps to keep the front end steering tighter and easier to adjust versus previous models. By enlarging

The king of the 82 series garden tractor was the 982. One of the most popular options on this tractor was the rear PTO and Category 0 3-point hitch. This rear shot of a 982 clearly shows these two options.

the spindle diameter, the 82 series could handle larger front-end loads over the most rugged terrain.

The cast-iron rear differential housing was retained from previous models for rugged durability. After the spin-off of the Cub Cadet line to Cub Cadet Corporation, the durable cast-iron rear differential housing (first used on the Cub Farmall) was replaced by more economical cast aluminum housing. Tipping the operators seat forward easily spots these cast aluminum housings, if a hydraulic oil level dipstick can be seen beside the battery, the tractor has the new style housing. Another method to identify which housing you have is to look at the paint color. Aluminum housings are painted black, cast-iron housings are painted red.

The 482 and 582 gear drive still used the reliable, and durable automotive style main drive clutch as the Quiet Line did. It did have some changes made to extend its life, such as a heavier drive plate and a new teaser spring for added reliability. The 482s were equipped with a creeper gear drive gearbox allowing it to have eight forward and two reverse gears. The 582 offered as standard equipment three forward and one reverse speed. Creeper gear drive box was an optional attachment. On both the 482 and 582, when the clutch pedal was depressed halfway, the tractor de-clutches; when fully depressed, the tractor brakes are applied.

Another nice feature of the 82 series that was commonly overlooked were the new rubber floor mats. You wouldn't be likely to slip in wet or icy weather with these new mats. The black color of the mats accents the styling of the 82 series. The spacious foot boards provide plenty of room to stretch out.

Blading gravel was easy with the front-mounted grading blade on this 82 series Cub Cadet. The 782's 18 horsepower engine helped get the job done fast.

A deluxe deeply padded vinyl covered seat is adjustable fore and aft to fit any operator. The new seat on the 82 series seat was thicker than the Quiet Line seats and featured a higher backrest for even greater lumbar comfort.

The 982 had an optional Category 0 3-point hitch and 2,000 rpm rear PTO available for the first time ever on a Cub Cadet. It has been stated by some that the 982 was IH's replacement for the Cub and 184 Cub Lo-Boy tractor.

All of the 82-series garden tractors could be outfitted with an optional, rear sleeve-hitch and hitch adapter. By using both the hitch and the adapter, a variety of sleeve-hitch-style implements (such as this garden plow) could be used for hundreds of tasks.

This is not true. When the 982 was introduced, it brought IH into a new market termed the super garden tractor. A Super Garden tractor was larger than a normal garden tractor, yet it was still smaller than the compact tractors being marketed.

The Super Garden tractors found great favor with larger estates, cemeteries, commercial lawn care businesses, and municipal/government agencies. The 982 shared many common components with its little' garden tractor brothers. The main difference in the

982 was the frame; it was longer. The difference can be easily spotted when measuring from the instrument support to the seat, on the 982's, the seat is about 5 inches back. The 982 also used a different steering wheel, similar to that found on the 184. An easy method to identify if the correct wheel is installed is to look at the steering wheel cap. The 982 has a round plastic cap with silver and blue bordering and a red/black IH logo in its center. The other model 82 series have a black triangular-shape plastic cap with a hot foil stamped silver IH emblem in them. Also, the 982 steering wheel had rounded spokes.

Another feature on the 982 was the dual brake pedal option. Two brake pedals located by the operator's right foot would control a disc brake mounted on each side of the rear axles. This would not only aid in steering, but provide better operation in loose ground. The clutch pedal on the left side of the tractor would still return the hydrostatic transmission to neutral when depressed fully. The dual pedal option was available as factory installed only.

Larger-diameter hydrostatic-drive transmission cooling fans were added to handle the higher horsepower of the 682, 782, and 982. The increased engine horsepower would cause the hydros to heat up quicker. Because larger tractors are worked harder for longer periods, it made larger cooling fans the only choice. The hydraulic lift cylinder also was improved with a new design of larger diameter, and larger capacity, that are easily serviced, unlike the previous throwaway-style lift cylinder. Stronger hydraulic lift and front hydraulic outlet control (optional) levers were also relocated to the left side of the dash to

An IH Scout, IH trailer, and an 82 series Cub Cadet are shown in this photo.

A popular rear attachment that IH sold was the #2B rear-mounted rotary tiller. This tiller was powered by a V-belt from the engine that was connected to a gearbox at the rear of the tractor. A fully enclosed drive and 38-inch-wide tilling cut blends soil and fertilizers to a depth of 7 inches.

Model	Engine	Engine horsepower	Transmission Type	List Price
182	Briggs	8	Gear	$1,926
282	Briggs	8	Gear	$2,176
382	Briggs	11	Gear	$2,389
482	Briggs	11	Gear	$2,465
582	Briggs	16	Gear	$2,880
682	Kohler	17	Hydro	$3,295
782	Kohler	17	Hydro	$3,760
982	Onan	19	Hydro	$4,885

reduce operator confusion with the hydrostatic transmission control lever.

At the tractors front end, new B-section PTO drive belts were used to provide longer belt life. The B-section belts offered greater horsepower capacity to reliably transmit the increased engine horsepower now available to the 82 series owner. The use of B section belts on the PTO clutch also necessitated the use of B-section pulleys on the various belt driven implements. You could use the older style A width pulley attachments on the 82 series but they would quickly eat the edges of the V-belt and destroy it prematurely. Older attachments that have the A pulleys on them can usually be converted to the B width pulley and vice versa.

On the early production machines, a mesh grille screen located behind the cast aluminum bar-style grille was included. Field use of the 82 series showed this screen collected debris and could cause an engine compartment fire or engine overheating. The screen was later dropped from production to allow foreign material to be blown out of the engine compartment and reduce the overheating and fire risk. The number of bars in the grille was also decreased to allow greater engine airflow.

To make the most of the new horsepower available to the 82 Series Cub Cadet owner, an improved series of mower decks was added. The model 38C (38-inch wide cut), 44C (44-inch wide cut), and 50C (50-inch wide cut) replaced the previous models 38A, 44A and 50A mower decks. The C series decks offered larger, rear gauge wheels for longer life and a larger drive pulley to accept the B-series PTO mule drive belt from the tractor. The dependable three-blade spindle mower drive was retained from the A series with the choice of standard or extra-hard coated blades available. The cutting heights could still be adjusted from 1 to 4 inch and of course, the free-floating action of the deck helps guard against scalping.

The many other attachments available on the prior model cub Cadets, including front mounted blades, lawn sweepers, landscape rollers, yard rakes, etc. were still retained with the exception of the two-post canopy with canvas top.

The lineup of front-mounted snow blower attachments was improved for the 82 series. The new models included the H36 (36 inch wide) snow blower for the 182, 282 and 382 Cadets and the H42 (42 inch wide) and H48 (48 inch wide) fit the 482, 582, 682, 782, and 982. The H stood for Haban Manufacturing Company of Racine, WI, who built the attachments; the corresponding number indicated the snow-blower width measured in inches.

A new PTO-driven rear-mounted tiller was offered to take advantage of the rear PTO and 3-point hitch option on the 982 Cub Cadet. The model 48 tiller was the perfect companion to a 982 outfitted with a rear PTO and 3-point hitch for the larger garden owner or commercial landscape operator.

The serial number is the last part of the model identification number and is preceded by the letter U, indicating the Cub Cadet was built in the United States.

CHAPTER 8

END OF THE LINE FOR THE CUB AND IH

The 1970s would mark the twilight hours for the Cub and Cub Lo Boy tractors. Increasing market competition in the compact tractor segment, coupled with an apparent lack of research and development by International Harvester (IH), and continually diminishing sales, would bring the 30-plus-year production run of the Cub to an end. The closure of IH's Louisville Works and subsequent sale of the Cub Cadet line to the newly formed Cub Cadet Corporation would be the outcome.

The Model 185 Cub Lo-Boy

The 185 Cub Lo-Boy would be the last yellow/white Lo-Boy tractor that IH would sell. It was styled similar to the 154, in that the hood and grille shell

The full line of IH outdoor power equipment that the company offered in 1980. The large range of tractors and equipment makes is quite clear that IH was serious about their consumer product line. The 184 Cub Lo-Boy and the 284 compact tractors would soon be retired, as would the line of rear-engine riding mowers, when IH sold off its consumer products line to Cub Cadet Corporation in 1981.

retained the same basic shape as the 154. The grille screen and hood striping was changed, along with the grille shell was painted white to match the hood. The front grille and headlight panel were black, and a single blue pinstripe paralleled the larger black stripe on the side of the hood indicating this was the Cub Lo-Boy 185.

The 185 was also IH's first High Horsepower Cub Lo-Boy. The IH-built 3/4 inch updraft carburetor found on the previously built 154 and all of the older Cub Lo-Boys and Cubs, was replaced by a new Zenith-brand carburetor featuring larger metering jets and a larger air filter-to-carburetor rubber air intake hose. Domed, cast aluminum pistons inside the engine helped burn the added fuel more completely. With more air and fuel in the engine, more horsepower could be created. The 185 also had the governed rpm limits of the engine adjusted upward to build more horsepower. The low idle speed was set at 600 rpm versus the 154's setting of 475 rpm. The high idle (2,510-rpm) and the rated load speed (2,300 rpm) were both boosted from the 154's settings of 2,420 rpm at high idle and 2,200 rpm at rated load speed.

By turning the engine faster more horsepower could be created. The downside to this was that as engine rpm increase the piston travel speed in feet per minute increases too. This increased piston speed translated into increased engine wear. In short, higher engine rpm meant faster engine wear. The 185 offered either a single or dual rear wheel brake pedals. The dual brake pedal kit was available as an optional extra cost item.

The 185 was painted IH 483 Federal Yellow in color on its chassis and rear fenders. The hood, grille housing, and wheel rims were IH 935 white. The upper and lower grille panels, footrest boards and steering column were painted IH black. The company located the serial number tag (part #166058C1) on top of the left frame rail near the front axle. This made identifying the tractor for service parts components much easier.

Nearly all of the implements offered with the 154 by IH were carried over into the 185's production too.

During its relatively short production span from 1974 to 1976, 6,346 International 185 Cub Lo-Boy tractors were built. The average retail price of a 185 Cub Lo-Boy in its last year of production (1976) was $3,820.

Serial Number Listings for International Cub 185 Lo-Boy Tractors	
37001 to 37315	Built in 1974
37316 to 41240	Built in 1975
41241 to 43347	Built in 1976

The New International Cub Tractor

In 1975, IH made the last major model change to the Cub tractor. This series was called the New International Cub Tractor (with increased horsepower). These Cubs started production in 1975 at serial number 248125 and continued until 1979 with the final serial number 253685, averaging out to 1,112 tractors built per year. This compares to the average of 20,388 Cub tractors made per year in the first ten years of the Farmall Cubs production. A drastic decline to say the least.

The new International Cub saw 5,560 units made making this one of the lowest production Cub tractor variations made. The styling of these Cubs remained unchanged from the previous International Cub except they had a long black pinstripe with a blue accent pinstripe.

The basic machine was still bathed in IH 483 Federal Yellow paint with the hood, grille shell, lights, and wheels painted IH 935 white. The operator seat was painted black. IH sold these Cubs with English, Spanish, French, and German caution/warning decals on them to meet the standards of the various export countries.

The New International Cub used the same basic engine specifications as the 154 Cub Lo-Boy tractor did. The increased horsepower was listed at 15 horsepower in IH sales literature. Yet, the 185 and 184 were produced with 18 horsepower engines. Why IH did not offer 18 horsepower engines in all three remains a mystery today. It is quite obvious that the 18 horsepower Lo-Boys could withstand the added horsepower in their drive train components.

IH continued to offer its Touch Control hydraulic system and its patented rear 1-point hitch called the Fast Hitch until the end of Cub production. IH was experiencing a high number of warranty claims on the hydraulic system, due to poor castings.

In 1978, IH offered three compact tractors to the market. The 15 horsepower International Cub, the 18 horsepower 184 Lo-Boy and the 28 horsepower model 284 compact tractor. The 200-series compacts that IH would introduce in the early 1980s replaced all three of these models. Due to the financial problems IH was

This overhead view of the 1970s vintage International Cub shows a 60-inch mower deck attached. Note the rear, diamond tread tires and multi-rib front tires that give minimal turf damage while giving maximum traction and steering control.

having, coupled with new proposed laws effecting exhaust emissions on tractors, it was clear that the International Harvester Cub was nearing its end. The last published list price of the International Cub was in 1979 and it listed for $5,350. Nearly 30 years later, some Cubs still command upwards of this price.

Serial Number Listings for New International Cub Tractor (with Increased horsepower)	
248125 to 248617	Built in 1975
248618 to 250831	Built in 1976
250832 to 252108	Built in 1977
252109 to 253135	Built in 1978
253136 to 253685	Built in 1979

The Model 184 Cub Lo-Boy

The model 184 Cub Lo-Boy brought the use of IH red paint back to the Cub tractor line. The 184 was styled after its big brother lineup of farm tractors, the IH 86 series.

The basic tractor was bathed in IH 2150 red, with IH 935 white wheel rims and side hood panels. A black

The International Cub is truly a tractor for all seasons. When outfitted with an International front-mounted grading blade, the Cub was ideally suited for winter snow plowing. Note the large cast-iron wheel weights added to the rear wheels to aid in traction.

decal stripe ran the length of the hood side and was similar in format and design to the larger IH 86 series agricultural tractors. The grille was styled as a scaled down version of the IH 686 tractor grille.

The characteristics of the C-60 engine on the 184 were similar to that on the prior model 185. Both used a Zenith updraft carburetor and had domed aluminum pistons. The 184's cooling system was identical to the previous models except for the radiator cap.

A newer Zenith carburetor that contained a revised needle valve and seat along with a larger orifice was added 2-28-77 at serial #43801. This change was made to overcome field complaints of the 184 experiencing vapor lock and stalling out found during prototype testing.

The C-60 engine in the 184, featured heavy-duty construction, designed to be long lasting. A cast-iron crankcase and cylinder head, along with a forged steel crankshaft that has induction hardened bearing journals (for long life) were standard issue on the 184. The engine main and connecting rod bearings featured an exclusive tri-metal design that allowed them to be serviced in the field with replaceable insert style bearings. Aluminum domed-top pistons with two compression and one oil ring were the same as those on the previous model 185. By using alloy-steel intake valves and silchrome-steel exhaust valves (with rotators on exhaust only) that were resistant to valve scorching, would allow the C-60 engine to still operate properly using unleaded fuel that was fast replacing regular gasoline. The lead in regular gasoline was used to lubricate the engine's valves.

Fingertip control of the hydraulic lift was easily within the operator's reach. The engine governor control lever was located directly next to this lever. Note the turnkey electric starting switch on this 1970s vintage Cub.

To keep the 184's running cool; the fan hub and blade assemblies underwent a major revision in September of 1979. The old-style fan/hub combination would now be offered as individual parts as a fan hub, and a fan blade assembly. The design of the fan hub was changed from an oil bath shaft, bushing and sheet metal pulley, to a new cast iron pulley and replaceable sealed ball bearing. This new style hub fit not only the 184, but also was retrofitted to the Cub, Farmall A, B, BN, A1, AV, AV-1, Super A and C agricultural tractors.

The earliest production 184's used the same combination starter/generator that the 185 model had. A new and improved starter generator first was installed on 11-8-77. This new starter/generator had a lighter weight frame, aluminum conductor field coils and an improved solenoid switch. At serial number 46112, IH began using a direct drive starter, which engaged a flywheel-mounted ring gear. This directly replaced the older starter/generator design with a separate cranking motor and alternator. A Delco 42-ampere alternator with an internal solid state regulator was added to handle charging. The 184's electrical system was a 12-volt.

One of the littlest parts that a person would expect to cause problems, did. The ignition key was prone to breakage. IH used the same ignition key in most of its tractors for parts commonality. The IH 86-series agricultural tractors had the ignition key handily positioned at operator knee height. When entering or exiting, (or just turning your body) your knee would hit the key. A similar problem arose in the 185 and 184 Lo-Boys. IH fixed this by replacing the thin key (#382458R2) with its new thick key (131313C1) at serial number 47045 on the 1978 production year model 184. The 131313C1 key had a stronger cross sectional area and is still used as the standard service part today.

Basic frame design of the 184 remained unchanged from the previous model 185 design until 12-13-77. IH modified the frame to accommodate the new flywheel-mounted starter. The flywheel shield was modified at this same date for the same purpose.

The transmission used on the 184 was identical to the previous model 185 except that the main-clutch drive shaft now used a universal joint at the transmission main shaft instead of a flexible disc drive coupler. The tractors main drive clutch was of a single stage design, meaning that if the pedal was depressed halfway down, the PTO would not disengage as in the 154 and 185. The clutch release bearing yoke was also improved over the 185 with a stronger Y shaped design used.

The 184s were equipped with a single brake pedal, but a two-pedal brake was available as a parts accessory. The 184 still used band style brakes, which contacted cast metal drums on final-drive differential shafts.

A creeper gear reduction drive gearbox was an optional attachment. This was recommended with the use of a front mounted snow blower or rear mounted tiller. This gearbox had to be manually engaged by a shifting lever with the tractors clutch pedal depressed to present gear clash. The creeper gear drive-box that was used on the 184 differed from the 154 and 185 in that it used a woodruff key to secure the U-joint to the creeper drive housing. Since the 184-transmission shaft drives with a woodruff key and the creeper drive output is pin drive, the transmission driveshaft also must be replaced when installing this attachment.

The 184 used a rear mounted electric clutch to activate the tractor PTO. This clutch was similar to that used in the current production Cub Cadet Garden tractors of the time. By using this, the operator could truly have an independent PTO. The main drive clutch no longer controlled all of the tractors PTO functions too. IH engineers noted that the possibility existed that the front and rear PTO shaft support bearings could fail at an early age. To correct this, the Independent PTO (IPTO) shaft diameter was increased, as was the related bearings at serial number 45004. The use of larger bearings also made to provide better bearing contact to the shaft. The PTO operated at full engine load speed of 1,880 rpm.

The competition offered garden tractors to compete against the 184 in the market place. IH was quick to capitalize on this and used the 184's advantages in advertising the better features that could only be found on the 184. To compete with the 184, John Deere offered its model 400. This was more of a super garden tractor in size than a compact tractor. The 400 more closely matched IH's soon to be released 982, than the IH 184. The Deere 400 was powered by a twin-cylinder air-cooled Kohler engine rated at 19.9 horsepower. Bolens offered its model HT23 that also was powered like the Deere with a Kohler twin cylinder, but it had an engine rating of a whopping 23 horsepower. Simplicity built both of its model 9020 and the Allis-Chalmers 720 tractor. These tractors were basically identical to each other except for the paint scheme, decals, and body styling (hoods). These two tractors were both powered by twin-cylinder, air-cooled Onan engines that were rated at 19.35 horsepower. All of these competitive models were gasoline powered and equipped with hydrostatic transmissions, hydraulic implement lift, and 12-volt electrical system. The Allis-Chalmers 720 and the Simplicity 9020 were the most comparable to the 184. They both were about the same size as the 184. The Bolens HT 23 and the 400 Deere were more scaled to the 982 Super Garden tractor that IH offered.

Even though the 184 was underpowered, when compared to the competition, it over powered them with its features that they lacked. With

The last of the Cub Lo-Boy series was the 18 horsepower model 184. Here, a 184 with a 60-inch IH mower deck makes the biggest yards look small in size. A water-cooled four-cylinder, model C-60 gasoline engine powered the 184. The hydraulic lift was standard equipment on the 184, and it made handling large implements easy with fingertip control.

The International Cub with an undermounted finishing mower got the largest mowing jobs done fast.

The Final Cub Tractor Line

In late 1978 or early 1979 IH made one last change to the iron horse of its tractor line, the International Cub. The exact date of this change alludes this author, but the change IH made to the Cub was to paint the entire tractor red. These all red Cubs were made in the tractors final months for reasons unknown. They still retained the long black hood stripe with it accenting blue pinstripe for styling, with a black grille screen. The later-printed owners manual shows a tractor similar to this, but IH never updated its sales literature or parts catalog to reflect this change. Maybe IH management knew the tractor was to be retired, or that the machine tooling was worn out and need to be rebuilt *again*. Hopefully more information on this last edition Cub will surface in the future to help explain this.

The One Arm Loader

No book on the Cub and Cub Lo-Boy tractors would be complete without mention of the most sought-after attachment for these tractors, the model 1000 hydraulic front end loader. This is commonly called the one arm loader amongst IH enthusiasts. This all-hydraulic loader was painted IH white and was made from 1962 to 1975. It actually was over-sized for the Cub with its loader frame attached to both the tractor rear axle and the front steering casting. A

an 8-gallon fuel tank, the 184 easy out-ran the Bolens HT 23, which offered only a 5-gallon supply. The 184 also offered an optional Category I rear 3-point hitch, all of its competitors could only offer a smaller Category 0 hitch. The competition out-ran the 184 in that they all were equipped with only a hydrostatic drive transmission versus the 184's three-speed gearbox. IH at one time investigated building a hydro Cub Lo-Boy, but never marketed one.

The marketing department at IH intended to sell the 184 primarily to commercial users such as landscapers and turf/grounds keepers. By stressing the advantages of IH's smooth running, water-cooled, efficient engine along with IH's famous durability, it would be natural to choose the 184. A key selling point was that IH's water-cooled engine lasted at least twice as long as those offered by the competitions air-cooled counterparts. Why sacrifice service reliability?

IH built 4,228 units of the International 184 Cub Lo-Boy in its 1976-1979 production. When compared to the 6,346 units of the prior model 185 built from 1974-1976, the 184 production was not record setting. This reduced production makes of the 184 which is highly sought after as a modern day collectible tractor. It is not uncommon to find 184 tractors selling for a higher price now than when they were new.

Model	Engine	Engine horsepower	Transmission Type	List Price
154	C-60	15	Gear	$2,405
185	C-60	18	Gear	$4,295
184	C-60	19	Gear	$5,650

separate control valve operated the loader using the tractor's hydraulic pump as its power source.

A Cub with a front end loader attachment can be a very useful machine, but the front axle, steering gearbox, and especially the spindles and narrow wheel rims used on the Cub greatly hindered the performance of this loader. The 1000 loader could easily overload the Cubs front axle and possibly cause the axle to break, and it could be installed on either the Cub or Cub Lo-Boy tractor.

The nickname one arm loader was given to the 1000 because it has only one loader lifting boom arm. Most front-end loaders have two parallel lifting arms. Another unique feature is the single hydraulic cylinder to tilt the bucket. The earlier style (1962-1965) used a metal pipe attached to the cylinder barrel. The models after 1965 used a cylinder with 90-degree elbows on the ends of the hydraulic hoses instead of the pipe. The model 1050A loader differed from the 1000 loader in that the 1050A was designed to fit the Cub Lo-Boy 154. The 1050A were built from 1970 to 1973 and used two loader-lifting arms and dual hydraulic cylinders to tilt the front bucket.

Closure of the Louisville Works Plant and Foundry

After more than 40 years in production and two major tooling changes (the machine tools and molds twice wore out), it was obvious that the Cub would be retired; to rebuild the Cub tooling for a third time would not be cost effective. The three major factors behind this decision were cost of production, replacing an aging production facility, and new engine emission regulations that were scheduled to take effect in the next decade which would mean a redesign of the engine. All three of these points plus others would seal the fate of the beloved Cub. Tractor manufacturers were turning to compact diesel powered tractors (usually built in Japan) for a fuel efficient, reliable, and clean-burning power source. Advancements in manufacturing and hydraulics had outstripped the Cub's design and marketability. IH's replacement for the Cub was a diesel powered compact sized tractor, built in Japan.

The drastic downturn in the North American agricultural economy in the early 1980s coupled with poor management decisions, and continued top heavy mismanagement; led to huge financial loses by International Harvester. Cash for physical plant revival was nonexistent. The Cub finally went into a permanent hibernation. IH had planned to build components of its new TR-4 and TR3 agricultural tractors at Louisville Works, but the economy and tractor sales both soured adding yet another nail into Louisville's coffin.

IH closed Louisville Works and transferred the Cub Cadet production line to its new facility in Brownsville, TN. The Louisville foundry and plant was eventually scrapped out and later razed. Today, the area that *was* the former Louisville Works is now part of the Louisville Airport.

The final-production Cub tractor was built in March 1979. In a notarized letter dated February 18, 1980, IH notified Miller True Value Hardware of Charlotte, North Carolina, that it was the recipient of the Final Production Cub Tractor. The letter states, "The International Harvester Company Louisville Plant began production of the Cub model in 1947. The customer acceptance of this product resulted in an amazing production record, which continued until March 1979. During the nearly 33 years this model was manufactured at Louisville, 245,831 Cub tractors were built."

The letter continues, "We are understandably proud of quality products produced at the Louisville Plant which have served the American Farmer and have contributed to his achievements. The end of an era for the Cub tractor was reached with serial number 253685. We congratulate you for being a part of this success story as the recipient of the last Cub tractor."

The final Cub was painted red and had a long blue stripe on the side of the hood, the same stripe its earlier yellow and white version had. The exact location of this final Cub eludes this author at the time of printing. One can only guess as to its whereabouts and current condition.

But the fact remains that the Farmall Cub is the longest running production tractor of all time.

Divestiture of the Cub Cadet Line by IH

With the closure of the Louisville, KY, plant by IH, the main source of Cub Cadet assembly was lost. IH had a new factory built in Brownsville, TN, to be the new replacement factory for the Cub Cadet's production. After much haranguing, IH executives decided to sell off the Cub Cadet line to a new independent company. This new company would be called the Cub Cadet Corporation (CCC). This new company was headquartered in Cleveland, OH, IH actually sold off its Outdoor Power Products line to Modern Tool and Die Company (MTD). A company was formed that was called Cub Cadet Corporation or CCC. The CCC was independent of the MTD brand, but MTD was the owner.

In a letter dated February 16, 1981, IH announced the new corporation to its dealer network:

Today we are pleased to announce a new manufacturing, marketing and distribution structure for Outdoor Power Products. A newly formed, independent company—called the Cub Cadet Corporation—has been formed. Effective June 1, 1981, they will manufacture the Cub Cadet line. Corporate headquarters will be at Brownsville, Tennessee, where fully integrated production of all components, sheet metal, etc., will be based. . .

As an independent company, the Cub Cadet Corporation will sell red lawn and garden tractors with the IH logo to International Harvester for marketing through its agricultural equipment dealers. They will sell yellow and white Cub Cadet tractors to current Outdoor Power Products dealers (J-120) who do not hold the agricultural contract.

The new company will be self funded, and will provide complete research and development, manufacturing, sales, merchandising and advertising support to all its independent Outdoor Power Products dealers. International Harvester will continue to provide full support to the product line sold through its agricultural equipment dealers.

Distribution of parts will be handled by International Harvester for both the agricultural equipment dealers and the independent Cub Cadet Corporation Dealers.

The new company will be able to produce high quality Cub Cadets with better production flexibility to match dealer demands. Shipments can be more timely scheduled to bring the right product to you when you want it. . .

The Cub Cadet Corporation is in place. As you read this, all elements of the program have been signed. It will be business as usual through June 1, 1981. As that date approaches, you will receive further communications with regard to (for the independent Outdoor Power Products dealers) transfer of contracts to the new company. . .

We believe the new organization will work to the benefit of all—to the dealer, our dealers, who have supported the business since the first Cadet garden tractor 20 years ago; to the International Harvester Company, which is now able to concentrate its business efforts toward the markets it knows best; to the Cub Cadet Corporation, which will specialize and grow in the outdoor power industry; and, most importantly, to your customer, who has available a premium product sold by the best servicing dealer network.

With an aggressive Spring Program in place, a hard hitting Direct Mail Program ready to launch and the best product line available, we look forward to your increasing sales, market share and profits. We seek your continued support to make this transition period as rewarding and smooth has possible.

–R. L. Lee, general manager, Outdoor Power Products

With this letter sent to IH dealers, the new Cub Cadet Corporation was born. IH was out of the consumer products market and was left to concentrate their efforts on trucks, and agricultural machinery. Ultimately, IH (later renamed Navistar, and now known as the International Truck and Engine Corporation) sacrificed its agriculture division to remain solvent and concentrate solely on engine and truck production.

CCC eventually became a division of the MTD Company that would become the largest manufacturer of outdoor power equipment. Today the Cub Cadet name still lives on. At the time of writing this book, the 40th anniversary of the Cub Cadet was taking place and a special-edition tractor was built. This one was painted to resemble the tractor that set the bar in the market of lawn and garden: The IH Cub Cadet Original.

INDEX